Wonderful Passaic

D1562092

7/23/2001

TO: HOWARD (PHS CLASS OF 1955)

I do hope you enjoy the book.

Bob

Other Books by Bob Rosenthal

Children's Book

When Papa Was Your Age

Non Fiction

Unbelievable

Wonderful Passaic

Memories and Recollections

Bob Rosenthal

Writer's Showcase
presented by *Writer's Digest*
San Jose New York Lincoln Shanghai

Wonderful Passaic
Memories and Recollections

All Rights Reserved © 2000 by Bob Rosenthal

No part of this book may be reproduced or transmitted in any form or by any
means, graphic, electronic, or mechanical, including photocopying, recording,
taping, or by any information storage retrieval system, without the
permission in writing from the publisher.

Writer's Showcase
presented by *Writer's Digest*
an imprint of iUniverse.com, Inc.

For information address:
iUniverse.com, Inc.
620 North 48th Street, Suite 201
Lincoln, NE 68504-3467
www.iuniverse.com

ISBN: 0-595-13047-X

Printed in the United States of America

Dedicated to my wife Carole who for 50 years has urged me to write stories about my Passaic friends.

Excerpts from the book "Passaic People 07055" are reprinted with permission of the author and copyright holder, Karen G. Tomczyk. They are shown in Italics.

Acknowledgment

"Special thanks to the many people who contributed to this book including: Ruth Sinberg Baker, a distinguished writer, whose suggestions to improve the readability of this book were invaluable; Morris Ellenbogen and Leonard Kronman, 'alumni' of Passaic, who checked many of the facts in this book and provided memories and suggestions.

"Their collective efforts were to insure all the events in this book are factual. However, if there are any errors, the fault is all mine."

—*Bob Rosenthal*

What is Passaic?

Passaic is a small city in New Jersey, thirteen miles west of New York City. It was part of the Acquackanonk Tract that was acquired in 1682 by Dutch families. By 1730 most portions of the present day Passaic, Clifton and Paterson had become farms of German and Dutch immigrants. It is where General George Washington spent considerable time during the Revolution (although his main army camped at Wayne, Pompton and Totowa, cities adjacent to Passaic). During the 1780's, Passaic County hired Charles L'Enfant to design the city of Paterson, of which Passaic was part of. However, his grand design was rejected as too costly and so he went off to another contract; i.e. the beautiful design of Washington, D.C.

Passaic (then known as Acquackanonk) separated from Paterson in 1831. The city incorporated and about 1873 changed its name from Acquackanonk. This was fifteen years after the Dundee Power Canal had built a 450 foot dam across the Passaic River to produce power. The canal and power from the dam brought industry to Passaic.

Passaic grew in the 1880's when the immigrant trains from New York stopped in Passaic bringing eager workers to the booming textile mills. The town of Passaic had about 1,000 residents in 1873, but had grown to about 28,000 people in 1900 and grew to its current population of about 60,000 in the 1940's.

Passaic is just 3.2 square miles in area. Although its population of 60,000 has remained essentially constant for over fifty years, the actual mix of people continues to change. Passaic is a true "melting pot community" where new immigrants seek the opportunities of America. Passaic is where my friends and I grew up during the Great

Depression and World War II. For most of us, our grandparents were born in Europe and emigrated to America as part of the great human flood of immigrants between 1880 and the 1920's. Our parents were born in America but still spoke the European language of their parents as well as English. Parents worked hard to support their families and only had one desire—that their children would succeed in America.

Passaic was loved and hated by my friends. We considered it dirty and old when we were growing up. We now realize it was perhaps the most beautiful, wonderful place to have ever lived in. It is the place where you developed friends that were friends for life. It's the place where you grew up and moved out of, thus making room for new immigrants and their dreams for their children.

Yes, Passaic symbolizes the very essence of the American dream—a place to be educated, a place to find initial employment, a place to mature and "graduate" to the full American experience.

Although this book provides a picture of this American "melting pot" from only one person's memories, it is hoped you will agree it is really the remembered youth of all of us.

So the answer to the question: What is Passaic? It was, and always will be, my wonderful hometown.

PART 1

Growing Up In Passaic

1932 to 1947

*"Daddy, before you spank me, I think you
should know that someday I'm going to write a book."*

CHAPTER 1

The Great Depression

Most of my classmates were born in the depth of the depression—in the year 1932. Of course, being a child during the depression was a lot easier than being an adult. As children we simply didn't understand the hardships and desperation people had trying to find work.

We didn't realize that there was great unemployment in the city of Passaic and we further didn't realize that some of the "games" that we played were because of the depression.

The Coal Truck Game

When I grew up I realized that my family was luckier than most others. My uncle owned a coal delivery company, and since every house was heated by coal in the 1930's, this provided a steady income for my uncle.

(For those that ever visit Passaic there is still a "monument" to my uncle's coal company. It is located in Passaic Park on Main Avenue just past Brook Avenue. It's a large concrete structure that used to hold coal cars more than ten feet in the air. The delivery trucks would pull up under the concrete structure and were filled with coal from the train's coal cars. Perhaps the reason it's still there is that some Passaic people must still believe that oil, gas or electric heating of homes is just a passing fad.)

My uncle, an immigrant from Russia, was in some ways a very benevolent man. He was happy to give jobs to his relatives. In other ways he was a tyrant. If you didn't perform the job the way he wanted, he'd fire you in a flash.

My father was very lucky. Although polio had crippled him, he knew how to drive a large coal truck and my uncle hired him.

It was about 1936 and I was four years old. I remember that my father's coal truck didn't have "inflatable tires." It had solid rubber tires and made an enormous noise when it was driven down the street because it shook at every bump. Adding to this noise was the chain drive transmission that provided power from the engine to the rear wheels.

Like everyone else, we heated our little "flat" using our own coal burning furnace located in the basement. However, as my mother always explained to me, coal costs money so we could not waste the coal. And because these were very tough economic times, my uncle absolutely forbade my father from giving us any coal to heat our house. He said my father would have to buy coal just like everyone else. Unfortunately, he didn't pay my father enough money to buy both food and coal. This "encouraged" my family to invent another way to get a small amount of coal so we wouldn't freeze in the New Jersey winter.

My sister, being four years older than me, went to school every day and would get home by 3:00 p.m. At 3:15 she and I carried a ten foot long piece of wood that was about four inches in diameter up from our basement. We also carried a large empty pail.

Our "flat," which was part of a four-family building, was located on a wide street (Oak Street) just after the bottom of the hill from the Lackawanna Railroad freight yard. We would stand on the side of Oak Street away from our house and watch the "Lackawanna hill" and wait and wait. Finally in the distance we heard a slight rumble—the noise that a coal truck was coming.

As the noise got a little louder we could finally see that the truck on the hill was the coal truck that my father drove. We would then quickly pick up the ten foot piece of wood and run into the street, drop it and run back on the sidewalk. We then stood back on the sidewalk as the coal truck came racing down the street and finally hit our wood "bump."

Well, since the coal truck did not have inflatable tires, it hit the wooden bump and the truck jumped up and fell back on the road in a giant bang, causing some coal to fall off the back of the truck.

My father would never stop. He didn't want to risk losing his job. He just kept driving while my sister and I would run out into the street, pick up the pieces of coal and put them into the pail. After we had cleared the street of the coal, we then picked up the wooden plank and the heavy pail, and brought them back to the basement. My mother would be waiting for us next to the furnace. She would then first "shake the grates," "put some coal in," "move the ball down" and "open the damper." In about twenty minutes this combination of actions would bring some heat to the noisy hot water radiators in our flat.

The remaining coal was dumped into our near empty coal bin, the pail and wood plank were put near the basement door, ready to be used again tomorrow at 3:15.

That's the way we heated our house in the cold winter of 1936.

*   *   *

When spring and summer came we no longer had to worry about how to heat our flat. However, a new overwhelming worry encompassed every family, particularly families with young children. That worry was the possibility of getting polio.

Of course, today we have vaccines to avoid the possibility of getting polio, but in the 1930's and 1940's this was perhaps the most dreaded disease there was. It was particularly true in my home because my father, when he was in his twenties, contracted polio which left him with a crippled left arm and other deformities. This haunted him for his whole life and affected our family's whole outlook towards polio. We were absolutely frightened of the disease.

Polio was very mysterious in the 1930's and 1940's. No one had any idea how you caught it. There were lots of wild rumors but there were no facts. Because of this lack of knowledge, there was no way to protect yourself from catching polio. Some of my friends' mothers would send their children to kindergarten (to my kindergarten) with large smelly pieces of garlic hanging around their necks. They were hoping the smelly garlic would scare away polio.

During the polio epidemic season (spring and fall), all public water fountains were covered and closed so people wouldn't risk getting polio if it happened to come in the water (which no one knew if it did). President Roosevelt, of course, had polio and he was an enthusiastic supporter of the "March of Dimes." During polio season, when we went to the movies (almost all kids went to the movies on Saturday afternoon), between the double feature, they would show a short film of President Roosevelt making an appeal for money for the March of Dimes. Then the movie would stop and the theater lights would be turned on. Ushers would pass around large buckets so people could donate money to the March of Dimes. We always donated even though money was very scarce.

Yes, polio had affected my father and left him partially crippled with a large hump back. He was only five foot two and weighed less than 100 pounds and was very self-conscious of it. Thus, he became an introvert, very shy, and didn't like to "stand out in a crowd."

In fact, let me relate a little story about his proudest moment that I know of. One day when I was about five, my father was able to borrow a car (we couldn't afford to buy a car at that time). We were driving down Passaic's Broadway towards Main Avenue when a large garbage truck cut in front of our car. My father leaned on the horn and pulled up along side the window of the garbage truck.

Looking out of our car window I could see that the garbage truck driver was a giant of a man. He and my father began yelling at each other. Since the car was much lower than the truck, the truck driver couldn't see my father, but I was standing up in the back and could see the truck driver. The yelling went on until finally the truck driver leaped out of the truck and my father in a rage leaped out of the car. They both ran around the truck, finally facing each other.

I'll never forget the truck driver's expression when he first looked at my father—this short little man with the crippled body. My father was screaming at the driver. The truck driver suddenly turned around and ran back into his truck and drove away. My father returned triumphantly to the car. He was so proud that the truck driver was obviously afraid of him, and instead of fighting, the truck driver ran away.

It was, I believe, my father's proudest moment because he proved to his family he could conquer anything. I was so proud of him.

*   *   *

In the depression, none of the kids had many toys. What this meant was that the few toys we had became incredibly valuable to each of us. I was lucky to have two metal toys. One was a dump truck that you could make the back go up and down, which I truly loved. But even more important, I had a small metal airplane that had a wing span of about six inches. Without question, it was my proudest toy and allowed me to dream of either being a pilot or maybe someday I would design airplanes!

I remember one special day at school, during afternoon kindergarten, in May of 1937, when we suddenly heard a commotion in the school hall. The teacher sternly marched over to the door to quell the noise. However, she discovered that the noise was from the principal, Mr. (Bill) Cruise, who was instructing all the teachers to take the children outside, that a stupendous event was happening.

The teacher quickly lined us up two by two holding hands and we marched out as if it was a fire drill. When we got outside we suddenly saw this giant "thing" in the sky. I had no idea what it was. It looked like it was just hanging there, but in fact it was moving very slowly.

It was the German dirigible "Hindenburg" which had flown non-stop from Germany, and was going to Lakehurst, New Jersey. We were told it was the world's largest flying machine (the length of almost three football fields). It was bright silver in color with a strange black and red symbol on its vertical tail. (In a few years we would learn to hate that symbol, the Nazi Swastika). It took a long time for the Hindenburg to pass over Passaic, but when it finally was out of sight we all went back into school and talked about it the rest of the day.

That afternoon I got drenched walking home in the rain. When I got to my house I excitedly told my mother about seeing the Hindenburg. She told me that she heard on our RCA Victor radio (in our living room) that the Hindenburg was zig-zagging over New Jersey to avoid the thunderstorms. She told me the bad weather had caused the Hindenburg to be very late in its arrival at Lakehurst, New Jersey. The scheduled landing time had been 8:00 a.m., but that it would now land this evening about 7:00 p.m. Moreover, she said that there was going to be a live radio broadcast describing its arrival.

Wow, not only had I seen the Hindenburg fly over Passaic, but I would also be able to listen to the radio describe its arrival in Lakehurst. I ran and told all the neighbors about the radio broadcast.

My father arrived home about 6:30 p.m. and, for the first and only time, we actually ate on the living room floor so we could hear the radio. I could hear all the flats in our building also had their radios turned on.

The announcer began describing that the Hindenburg was slowly approaching the Lakehurst landing area. He described how beautiful it looked and how large it was (over 840 feet long). He then said that the Hindenburg had released its landing lines and the ground crew had attached the first line to a powerful winch. Suddenly the announcer started screaming that the Hindenburg was on fire, and the total airship was in flames. The announcer started to cry saying this was "the worst catastrophe in the history of the world."

We were all also crying. I just couldn't believe that that beautiful airship I had seen that afternoon had disappeared in a giant fireball.

For the next few days, all anyone talked about was the Hindenburg disaster, and about the miracle that only 13 of the 72 passengers died (a total of 36 were killed; 13 passengers, 22 air crew members, and one of the ground crew).

There were many investigations of this accident but they never proved what caused the fire. Even 64 years later, in the year 2000, a NASA expert announced a new theory of what had caused the Hindenburg disaster.

The Hindenburg explosion ended the era of airships. Never again would Germany use its resources to build such an exquisite means of travel. Moreover, the United States also stopped building these wonderful lighter-than-air ships of the sky.

*   *   *

As I grew a little bit older, about age six, I heard my parents talk about the possibility of war in Europe. I also noticed pictures in our local newspaper of Americans marching in Long Island and New Jersey with wooden sticks shaped like rifles. They didn't have uniforms but had arm bands with the same symbol I had seen on the Hindenburg, the Swastika, which I now knew stood for Hitler and the worries of war in Europe.

My parents explained that these were a minority of Americans whose parents or grandparents had emigrated from Germany and they were called "The German-American Bund." They pointed out that we, as Jews, had to worry about this kind of activity. However, they also pointed out to us that we were not unprotected; we would be protected by President Roosevelt. If that failed, we had "our own means." A few months later I learned what "our own means" meant.

✳   ✳   ✳

Each wave of immigrants that came to the United States was composed of many hardworking people. All they wanted was to have a better life for their children. But with each immigration wave—whether it was the Irish, the Italians, the Hungarians, the Jewish or others—a small part of them became gangsters and formed their own criminal organizations.

Among the Jewish gangsters were the famous Meyer Lansky, Bugsy Siegal, and the Purple Gang in Detroit. But there were many other Jewish gang leaders including my mother's first cousin Morris Feinberg.

While I'm not going to apologize for my cousin or for any of the other Jewish criminals, they should never be forgotten. Why? Because they were also patriots.

For example, The Passaic Herald News reported that in a city adjacent to Passaic, a well advertised rally for the German-American Bund rally was held in a large hall. There were many speeches made by their leaders, speeches that were very anti-Semitic wherein their leaders encouraged their members to beat up Jews and destroy Jewish property. That went on for about forty-five minutes according to The Herald News. At about that moment, my cousin and his "lantsmen" (his gang whose parents emigrated from the same town in Russia) broke into the hall, and to everybody's astonishment, they fought their way up to the speaker's platform and beat up all the leaders of the German-American Bund. Then they picked up these leaders and carried them through the crowd and threw them out on the sidewalk. When they did this no one in the large audience helped these leaders. They all began to file out and disappear and go home.

That was the last meeting of the German-American Bund in any city near Passaic.

Yes, my cousin and his associates were gangsters but we all appreciated that they were also patriots. I now understand what my mother meant when she said, "We have our own means."

    *   *   *

My mother was a typical Jewish housewife. She didn't have a job outside the home and took care of the family and the home. She of course didn't drive because at that time almost no women drove. And like all mothers, she was gentle and kind, and of course I loved her dearly.

But there was another side of her that I never knew about until one night at about three in the morning when I was about eight years old.

I was asleep in my bed (I had to share my room with my older sister) when we heard a loud knocking at the door. My mother and father got up and so did my sister and I. However, we just peaked around the door. When the door was opened there was my cousin Morris, carrying a large shopping bag. My mother and father were surprised to see him but perhaps they weren't unduly surprised.

Morris quickly came in and locked the door behind him. He then told my mother that he had just finished having the luckiest streak he ever had in a crap game and had won over $100,000 and all this money was in the shopping bag.

I remember thinking $100,000, how could that be? I got an allowance of two cents a week and the rent we paid was only $35 a month and no one could have $100,000.

He opened the bag and showed us that he did have it. Then he told my mother that he was afraid of going home with the bag because he knew there would be people waiting to rob or kill him if he had the loot with him. He asked my mother would she guard it, he'd be back by 11:00 a.m. in the morning with his body guards to pick up the money.

My mother nodded yes and walked over to the cupboard where our good dishes were stored. She climbed up on the kitchen counter and reached behind the good dishes and took down a pistol and a box of shells. (I never knew there had been a gun in our flat.) She sat down at the kitchen table and professionally opened up the pistol, cleaned it, put six shells in its chambers and closed the pistol. She then told Morris that he shouldn't worry, she'd stay up and guard the money. He thanked her and left. My father asked if he should stay up. She said, "No, you've got to go to work in a few hours." So he went back to sleep. Both my sister and I went back to bed but I couldn't sleep all night, worrying.

I got up about an hour earlier than I would usually get up, about 6:30 in the morning, and there was my mother, eyes wide open, sitting at the kitchen table with the gun in her hand. Right next to her was the shopping bag, obviously never again opened.

She then got up and put the gun into her housedress pocket, made me breakfast, kissed me goodbye and got me off to school. As I was leaving the house I noticed she was again sitting down at the table, having taken the gun out of her dress and holding it in her hand.

Later I learned that my cousin did come back with his two "gorillas" that were his usual body guards and picked up the money. He thanked my mother profusely and gave the family $25 which my mother thought was incredibly generous. I didn't know what to think knowing that he had $100,000.

And I never again saw the gun although I was sure my mother had again hidden it in our house.

*   *   *

At school that day I changed my usual routine. In art class I always attempted to draw pictures of airplanes, either the outside of airplanes or the interior of airplanes. Although I couldn't draw well (I could never color between the lines) I really enjoyed art class.

Except that day.

Because on that day instead of drawing pictures of airplanes I drew a picture of a woman sitting and holding a gun. My teacher, whose name I clearly remember as Mrs. Enema (but other people claimed her name was Mrs. Venema), stopped as she was passing my desk and said that she was surprised that I was drawing such a picture instead of my usual airplanes. I refused to look up and I refused to answer her. I just kept on coloring the gun black.

*   *   *

Of course my father and mother knew I was infatuated with airplanes. On Sunday afternoons we often went to the Museum of Modern Science in New York so I could see the various airplane exhibits. The museum was always great, but not as great as what occurred a few years before.

*   *   *

The year was 1936 and although the country was still in the depression, my father no longer drove the coal truck. Instead he and his brother had recently opened up a small men's clothing store on the corner of Monroe Street and Lucille Place, an ethnically diverse part of Passaic. It was about two blocks from my public school. The store was called "Moe and Morris." The only time my father was ever off from work was on Sunday afternoons.

Except for one very special Saturday morning.

My father had been telling me for weeks that a miracle in the sky was going to occur on a Saturday morning, and that he knew I would want to be there to see this miracle. Of course, I was very excited. However, my enthusiasm disappeared when he told me that he would wake me up at five in the morning so we would have plenty of time to get there. It didn't help much that my sister told me that waking up at five in the morning was very dangerous. She said there would still be ghosts and boogie men around from the previous night.

But on that magic Saturday morning my father did manage to wake me up. The whole family piled into a borrowed car. In fact, the previous night I helped carry pails of water from our sink on the second floor to wash the car so it would be ready for this monumental day.

We got in the car and off we went to Teeterboro Airfield about ten miles from Passaic. (There were no "airports" in 1939. They were called airfields.) Also, there were no real highways in 1939. Thus, we had to drive on narrow two lane roads and even though it was very early in the morning there was a lot of traffic, all going in our direction.

It took us about an hour to get to the airfield. When we arrived we found that an enormous crowd was already there, perhaps the largest crowd I'd ever seen. We parked the car and all of us ran to the edge of the single runway. We could see a band playing. Everybody was happy and jovial. I begged my father to tell me what was going to happen. He said, "Just wait, you'll see."

I couldn't wait. I couldn't imagine what this great event was going to be.

A little while later somebody shouted and pointed to a tiny spec of light in the sky and yelled, "THERE IT IS!" The entire crowd roared. I even roared although I had no idea what this was all about. My father roared, my mother roared, everybody roared. We watched the speck of light that began to get bigger and bigger. Finally, I realized it was an airplane, no not an airplane, a giant airplane; not a giant airplane, a super giant airplane, bigger than any airplane ever in history.

Finally, the airplane flew over the airfield and the band played and the people let balloons go and everybody cheered and jumped up and down. Then the airplane made a slow circle and landed and taxied right in the middle of the runway near us and stopped.

It was amazing. This airplane was silver and had two large wheels in its main landing gear under the wing and a little wheel under the tail. Painted on its side was "American Airlines." It was enormous.

The band was playing. Then the airplane door opened and a beautiful uniformed lady stood at the top of the stairwell. The crowd went crazy yelling.

She then stepped aside and began to allow people to climb off the monstrous airplane. As each person came down the stairs, everyone in the crowd yelled at the same time, "1", "2." The crowd got louder and louder as the number just kept going up and up. We counted "10," then "11." We couldn't believe that so many people could be on an airplane, and then "15" and even "20," and finally the last passenger got off. Twenty-one passengers in one airplane! Never before was there such an airplane and we thought never again will there be another airplane like this.

The airplane was the DC-3, the first time a commercial airliner had flown across the United States carrying passengers. It had completed the flight from California in an unbelievable two days. Even more fantastic, the airplane had to land only five times between California and New Jersey to refuel. Incredible!

And just as incredible, the airplanes top speed was 120 miles per hour. It flew at 8,000 feet altitude—more than one and one half miles high in the sky. It was amazing! My father told me that never before had so many people moved from such far places at such high speed in such a short period of time. My father was right. This was really a miraculous day!

Let me apologize to the readers of this book. I know you may not think it was such a miracle or even maybe not such a big deal. But you must remember that was 1936. Yes, and of course today we have jumbo jets that hold more than 400 people. Yes, they can fly over 8,000 miles non stop and yes they fly eight miles high. But that is today. Yesterday in 1936 I hugged my father and thanked him for waking me up at the ungodly hour of 5:00 in the morning when my sister said that the ghosts and boogie men were still awake. As we drove home I had convinced myself that some day I would design airplanes—after we got home I was so excited that I rushed to tell all my friends. After bragging about this, particularly to my friend Moishe who didn't go, I went home and decided I would splurge one of the two pennies that I had been holding in my secret saving place.

*   *   *

We lived near the edge of a Jewish section in Passaic's Second Ward. If you went up Hammond Avenue from where we lived there were mostly Italians. If you would have gone about one and one half blocks south towards Main Avenue on Oak Street, that would be the street of what was called the "Negro neighborhood." (Of course, there were no written rules where you could live in Passaic, but everybody sort of knew where you could live.) Separating the Jewish and Negro neighborhoods was a large old building that looked like a garage. In the back of that building was one of the most wonderful places in the city of Passaic. It was where they made fresh donuts every night for delivery in the morning.

Not only were they donuts, they were unique donuts with hard sugar on the outside, that were filled with either cream or jelly. Certainly, my favorite was jelly.

Their price was three donuts for five cents. Of course, I never had five cents at one time and I would never think of spending both pennies I had saved even for a wonderful donut.

However, on special occasions, like the day that I saw this giant airplane, I would be willing to spend a penny.

Thus when sundown came, after bragging about seeing the DC-3 to all the boys under the street lamp where we usually met, I walked the block and a half and stood outside the door of the donut factory. I waited and waited until I saw two kids walking towards the door. As they got to the donut factory door, I asked what they were buying and they each said they were getting a jelly donut.

When they opened the door I walked in right behind them. The factory was laid out so there was a desk near the door where you paid your money (most of the factory business was delivering to the various grocery stores the next morning; however, they did sell to whoever walked in the door). The aroma of the donuts being cooked in oil was a heavenly smell (the memory of which I still cherish today). The first kid put down his two cents and said he wanted a jelly donut, the second kid put down two cents and said he also wanted a jelly donut. Then I walked over and put down my penny and said, "Three for five. I want a jelly donut."

The man looked up. He knew me and he knew just what I was doing, but he gave a half smile and took the penny. He then let us walk over to where the donuts were being cooked, and as soon as a fresh batch was ready he reached in and took out three hot donuts. He put one of the donuts on the little nozzle at the end of the jelly pump and pumped it once and handed it to the first boy. He then placed the second donut on the same nozzle and pumped it once and gave it to the second boy. As soon as they got their donuts they began eating and walked out. He then picked up my donut and put it on the pump and pumped it four times. It looked like it would explode in a second. He smiled, gave me a large napkin, and the swollen jelly donut. I thanked him profusely.

Can you imagine! On the same day that I saw the world's largest airplane I also had a super spectacular hot fresh fully stuffed jelly donut.

Perhaps the best day of my life.

*   *   *

And that night in our bedroom I crossed my fingers on both hands and turned to my sister and said, "There are no such things as boogie men and ghosts" and stuck out my tongue at her. I then rolled over on my side and fell sound asleep and had wonderful dreams. When I woke up, my fingers were still crossed. They had protected me from the boogie men and ghosts.

CHAPTER 2

Learning About Sex on the Street Corner

In the 1940's Passaic had a great public school system. Even in grammar school and junior high it provided such classic courses as Latin, Shakespeare, classical music and the Renaissance. It also provided practical courses such as woodworking, textile production, printing and even automotive repair. But for the boys, it did not provide any sex education courses. We learned about sex the right way; from the older boys on the street corner.

And on that street corner we often speculated on what secrets the nurse at Public School Number 11 (Memorial Junior High School) was teaching the fifth and sixth grade Health Class which was for girls only.

But that's ahead of my story. First some history.

October 17th

Whenever October 17th occurs, it tends to make me think back to my youth in Passaic—the 1930/40's where many happy events occurred, and when sometimes an event that really was tragic.

October 17th was the day that one of my closest childhood friends was born. She was born two days after me, and her crib was next to my crib in Passaic's General Hospital. Not only that, but when she left the hospital I discovered that she lived in the house next to mine. Her name was "G".

My earliest recollections are of playing with G. This was the time of the Great Depression where everybody was out of work and although I didn't realize it, both her family and my family were poor. No, that's not really true. Actually, as a child I thought her family was as rich as the Rockefeller family.

They had to be Rockefellers. I lived in a walk-up tenement. They lived in a two-story house. Could you imagine only one family in a whole house! I had no back yard. They had a fenced in back yard—a real fence around real grass. Certainly that was evidence of being the Rockefellers and as even further evidence, G's father had installed a large swing set in the back yard. Her own swing set! No one I knew ever had such wealth.

Just after G and I turned nine, the Second World War started, and government "rationing" was imposed on almost all consumer purchases including on the amount of gasoline you could buy. There were four rationing classifications. An "A" classification, which could be had by almost anyone, entitled the holder to four gallons a week. The "B" classification was worth about eight gallons a week. "C" was reserved for important folk, like doctors, and the magic "X" went to people whose very survival required that they be able to purchase gasoline in unlimited quantities. My family had the lowly "A" sticker on our car window.

As further evidence of G's family's incredible wealth, her father had a truck with a magic "X" gas ration sticker on his window which meant that he could buy an unlimited amount of gas. It was rumored that President Roosevelt didn't even have an "X." Thus, it was obvious that her father had an important "position" to help the war effort.

This position involved improving the hygiene in the city of Passaic. Her father (I know you're not going to believe that anybody could possibly have such a wonderful occupation) drove a laundry truck—a truly amazing occupation.

When G and I became five years old, we went to the same kindergarten. As we grew up together, we had many adventures. For example, the street in front of her house (Paulison Avenue) led up a giant hill to the city's incinerator (yes, we really lived in the best part of town). Each afternoon the town's street cleaning trucks would go up to the incinerator to empty their load.

I remember it like it was yesterday, G and I each afternoon running down to the curb and yelling to the men driving the street cleaners, "DO YOU HAVE ANY BALLS?"

The street cleaners in our town always had these great smiles on their faces when we yelled. They always seemed to adjust their pants in a funny way (today with TV, everybody has seen baseball players do the same funny adjustments to their pants). But invariably the driver would reach into the bin under the hood of the street cleaner and would throw us old tennis balls that had been swept up in their daily toils.

As all of you surely remember from your own childhood, the ages between six and maybe eleven were astounding years. You learned to read, to go to school by yourself, to be able to do many things. Well, G helped me learn all those things. She even taught me how to tie my shoe laces. We were inseparable.

Also, many of you might remember pin-up posters of the Second World War, particularly the famous one with Betty Grable which showed the back of her legs and the outline of her pointed bosom. I must admit I had a secret that I didn't share with G. I was always intrigued about how the bosom of Betty Grable was able to stick out so straight and come to a point.

The only other thing I really knew that came to a point like that were the paper "soda cups" used in the candy stores during this time period. The early 1940's were a time of fear of TB and polio epidemics. Because of that, candy stores sold sodas in paper cups shaped as cones that fit into metal holders. Because of my secret intrigue concerning bosoms I often took these paper cones home and squashed them under my foot to see how they got such strength to remain pointed. My conclusion was of course, that Betty Grable must have had some type of cone bone structure that provided such rigidity.

Of course I never discussed this with G, but I did think about it.

Then came that fateful day. We were about eleven years old, the closest of friends. G had matured much quicker than I had. She was much taller (I was just a skinny runt).

One of our favorite games was playing tag. Although she was bigger than me, I was faster, and therefore, in this game I could hold my own. Many of our friends were playing with us and G was "it." Maybe because I was her favorite, she chased me and caught and tagged me and I became "it." After the appropriate time interval, I began chasing her again to tag her. As I began to catch up to her a disaster occurred, a disaster that would haunt me for more than fifty years.

G tried a new tactic. She decided to turn around, raise her hands and scare me (remember she was bigger than I was). As she turned around, I was just reaching to tag her back. I couldn't stop running although she had just stopped running, and I tagged her, not in the back, but in her bosom.

I remember that instant still today. Time didn't stop but it went into very slow motion. My hand began to sink into her bosom and it sank further and further and further. My mind went crazy. Like giant headlines in the newspaper, my mind said I JUST SQUASHED G's TIT.

In the slow motion I saw her face become enraged. I turned and ran for my life and hid in the coal bin in my basement. She searched for me screaming but didn't find me.

As previously mentioned, in the 1940's Passaic schools didn't have sex education programs. You learned about sex the proper way—out with the guys at night under the street light talking about girls. In my neighborhood most of the boys were a little bit older than I was. Thus, I tended to do a lot more listening than talking.

As I went upstairs in my house, I was still shaking from the tag catastrophe. I couldn't remember what the result of such an action was. I knew from prior discussions with my friends under the street light, that if you touched a girl "there" you either gave her cancer or made her pregnant, but I didn't remember which one it was. I counted the minutes for the sun to set so that I could rush out to the street corner and find out the fate that I had given to G.

Nighttime finally came. I ate dinner in a frenzy, didn't say a word to my mother and father, ran downstairs and "nonchalantly" wandered over to the street corner. The guys were beginning to gather and the subject, of course, always got around to girls. As I previously mentioned, I normally didn't participate, I almost always just listened. But tonight I had to find out what I had done to G. I was embarrassed, I was ashamed, I was overwrought, but I managed to ask the question (of course without mentioning G's name) in a way that I thought was nonchalant.

Immediately my friends spun around and faced me. One turned to the other and said, "I think Bobby felt-up a girl today." Another one looked at me with sudden found envy and respect. Suddenly, instead of being the little guy that was always listening, I was a hero. The guys pounded me on the back and wanted to know details. I, of course, knew the secret of being a hero. Never tell any details because people's imagination is always better than any details you could tell them. So I answered them by saying, "I can't talk about it" and other similar noncommittal statements. That night I never did learn what I had done to G. Was it cancer, or was she going to be pregnant?

*   *   *

It is now more than fifty years since that incident and I remember it like it was one minute ago. That one incident certainly changed my life for the worst. Because of that one incident, G and I never talked to each other again. I was afraid to talk to her and I assume she was frightened of the sex-hungry monster that had made believe he was playing tag, but was really attempting to mutilate her.

Although G and I graduated from high school together, I can't recall us ever even looking at each other, let alone talking again. And yet, G was and always will be my closest girl friend.

I don't know where G is today, except I know that part of her is always in my heart. I miss my Passaic childhood desperately. I miss the fun of playing on her swings. I miss standing on the curb yelling at the street cleaners. I miss G.

So wherever you are, G, I hope some day you read this and recognize whom I'm talking about. If you do, please daydream back to our wonderful times before the terrible event occurred.

CHAPTER 3

Number 11 School

In the 1930's and 1940's Passaic used the concept of "community schools." Thus, you went to a school that was within walking distance of your home. There were no school buses and you walked home for lunch every day and had to be back in time for the afternoon session.

In fact, there were no school buses anywhere in the city of Passaic, not even for the high school. Wherever you lived in the city, you walked to the high school.

We lived three long blocks from Number 11 School which was a great modern school. It was an imposing three story structure built in the late 1920's. Thus, at the time I went there it was rather new. It was built as a memorial to all the Passaic men who were killed in the "Great War" (which is now called World War I). The lobby of the school—which the students were never allowed to visit or walk through—contained a memorial to those fallen soldiers and a closed coffin. It was commonly rumored that any student that didn't instantly obey their teacher would be placed in the coffin. Obviously, we all obeyed our teachers.

The school had five different entrances. The front entrance next to where the beautiful flag pole stood was the main lobby, the forbidden entrance to any student. Going clockwise around the building was the Kindergarten Entrance adjacent to a large playground where all the young children had enormous fun before school and at lunch time. Around the next corner of the school was the entrance to the Grammar School; for the first through fifth grades. It was used by both boys and girls (as was the kindergarten entrance). It led primarily to the second floor where most of the "grammar school grades" had their class rooms. Just after this doorway was the special boiler room building including its giant smoke stack where the coal fed burners were used to keep the school warm. On the other side of the boiler room building was the Boys' Junior High Entrance. Junior High included grades seven through ninth grade (high school was tenth, eleventh and twelfth grades only). For some reason, that we didn't understand, girls were not allowed either to play in the Junior High boys' area or to walk through the boys' doors.

As you went around the building from the boys' entrance, at the far end was the Girls' Junior High School Entrance. Unlike the boys' entrance which had a concrete playing area, the girls had a grass playground. Obviously, we boys believed that the girls had to have the grass because they were more dainty than we were.

We were all extremely proud of Number 11 School. We were proud that on the first floor there were two wonderful gyms, a boys' gym and a girls' gym. They were located on either side of a large modern auditorium which included a balcony so that all the students in the school could attend a common assembly. The auditorium had a fully operational stage with foot lights, overhead lights, moveable curtains, etc.

The first floor also contained the library, the two kindergarten rooms, the nature study room, as well as the various "shops" where printing, automotive repair, textile weaving, and other skills were taught. The next two floors contained classrooms that surrounded a central area which also was subdivided into classrooms.

Perhaps it sounds strange but three of the "modern" conveniences in the school truly impressed all visitors in the 1930's. First, there was a common vacuuming system that had ports in every classroom and in the halls. You would simply lift up the port, insert the cleaning apparatus and the vacuum would suck all the dirt away. Second, in the administrative and principal's offices, located on the second floor, there was a giant pendulum clock that kept the master time for the school. Each classroom had a smaller pendulum clock that was a slave to this one master clock. If the master clock stopped all the classroom clocks stopped. This almost never happened. But it did stop in 1945 (more about this later). Third, each classroom had a small telephone built into the wall that directly connected to the secretary in the principal's office. This was considered amazing since almost no one even had a telephone at home.

*   *   *

Of course, our school did not have computers, televisions, cafeterias, internet, or air-conditioning. But it did have one thing: Very Strict Teachers!

And if you did anything wrong, the teacher would grab you by the ear and drag you down to Mr. Cruise's office on the second floor. Mr. Cruise, it was rumored, had the legal right to rip your heart right out. Obviously, no one ever wanted to go to the principal's office. Of course, in 1939 I was a perfect boy and never did anything to get the teachers angry. At least I tried not to let the teacher see me when I did things that would get her angry. But sometimes "accidents" do happen.

For example, on each desk there was a little hole in the top right hand corner. In this hole would be a small glass bottle with a hole in its top. Into that hole you would pour wet, liquid black ink. This allowed each student to use a terrible "pen" provided by the school to write with. I was convinced this was the same "pen" that was used to write the Declaration of Independence (ball point pens weren't invented until after the Second World War).

If the teacher thought you were an outstanding student she would select you to go around and fill up all the ink bottles on the desks from a giant ink bottle kept in the corner of the room. Well, since I was such a perfect boy, one day she picked me. I couldn't believe that I had received such an honor. I was so proud! I picked up the giant bottle with a big smile on my face and I could see all my classmates were jealous. I walked over to the first desk and took the top off the big ink bottle and then it happened. I DROPPED THE BIG INK BOTTLE!

It smashed on the desk, splattered on the floor, on the walls, on the girl that sat in front, on the girl that sat behind, on the girl that was at the desk, on the boy that was on the left side and on the big bully that always beat me up who sat on the right side. Of course, the ink was also all over me.

I quickly got the feeling that maybe I had done something wrong. Now there are many things you can do when you think you've done something wrong and the teacher is charging up the aisle to grab your ear and drag you down to the principal who might rip your heart out. At the same time, the big bully was angry and I really believed I could see smoke coming out of his nostrils. I decided I would then do the honorable thing.

I ran like hell, with the broken half bottle of ink still in my hands, dripping, from the classroom, down the hall, down the stairs, through the forbidden front lobby of the school until I finally got outside and realized that I had "inked" the entire school. I could hear the explosion of people screaming at me. I could almost feel the people chasing me.

Fortunately, at age seven I was a fast runner and I ran the three city blocks to my home. I quickly took off the ink covered clothes (and of course, hid them from my mother) and put on clean clothes. I washed up and then I ran as fast as I could back to the school. I then ran into the school through the Girls' Entrance, and snuck up the back stairway. Fortunately, no one was in my classroom so I went into the room and sat at my desk.

Where was everybody in my class? They were all out in the hall trying to clean up the ink mess and I just sat there waiting for them to come back. Finally, my friend Moishe came back to the class. He in his most kindly way said, "Bobby, you're dog meat." I didn't think he was complimenting me. Then the whole class came back. They were full of ink and had hatred for me in their eyes. The teacher walked in also covered in ink and was very angry. Then she spotted me there in my clean clothes sitting at my desk.

At that same instant the school's principal—Mr. Rip Yourheartout—stormed into the classroom. He yelled at the teacher and said, "Miss Kowalski, who dumped the ink bottle throughout the school?" She pointed the finger at me. The principal asked me to stand up. Trembling I stood up. All eyes were on me. The bully had the smirk of watching me face imminent death. Then the principal said, "It couldn't have been Robert. He is the only one with clean clothes on in this classroom." My teacher said, "But, but, but…" The principal cut her off and said, "It must have been" and pointed at the bully and demanded that the bully come with him. The bully looked at me with even more hatred in his eyes. I think steam was not only coming out of his nose but also out of both ears.

There really must be a God because when the bully returned from the principal's office, he had a small smile on his face, and waved a happy wave in my direction.

No one in the class said anything. No one asked him the obvious question (had his heart been ripped out)? The bully turned to the teacher and said, "The principal suggested we get on with our mathematics." The teacher first said, "But, but, but…" Then she decided she better start the lesson (or maybe the principal would rip her heart out). The class went on like it was a normal day. However, I knew the school day was going to end, and then I'd have to walk out with my classmates and with the bully who was still full of ink.

Finally, the bell sounded and we all walked down the stairs of the three story school. As we got out into the school yard I was prepared for one of the fastest runs I had ever made. I kept one eye on the bully but he was friendly to me. In fact, he came over and said, "Wasn't it an exciting day?" He then asked if I'd like to play on his baseball team. I was amazed. Obviously, something the principal had done or said had fundamentally changed him. But obviously, I didn't ask him about it because I didn't want to get him angry by reminding him he was still covered with ink.

I didn't know what the principal had told him until thirty years later when I happened to accidentally meet the same "bully," except he was no longer a bully. He was now the principal of a school of another city in New Jersey. I finally worked up the courage to ask him if he remembered the ink bottle incident in Number 11 School. With a big smile he said, "I certainly do." I then asked him what happened when he went to Mr. "Rip Yourheartout's office" that day.

He leaned back, still smiling, and he told me he had promised the principal never to discuss it, but maybe now is OK because thirty years had passed. I said, "So, what happened when you went to the principal's office?" His answer was, "The principal explained to me that he knew that you spilled the ink bottle. He said you would forever worry that the principal might find out. He said that your worrying forever was your punishment and that your punishment was worse than the threat of having your heart ripped out."

I then asked him, "Then why did you suddenly become my friend and ask me to play on your baseball team?" He explained, as if I was still seven years old, that the reason he did it is the principal convinced him that if he treated me like a friend he would get to be popular in the school. You see, he really didn't want to be a bully and the only reason he was a bully was because he had no friends.

So aren't we all lucky today that there are ballpoint pens and there are no longer big ink bottles that need to be used to fill the little bottles on the desks! And aren't we now lucky that schools have air conditioning and aren't we lucky that there are school buses and cafeterias and over-head projectors and all those things! But even with all those modern things that are in schools today, still the most important thing you could ever have in school are good friends, because good friends last your entire lifetime.

And that was probably the most important thing I learned when I was seven years old.

* * *

The following actually happened fifty years **after** I was in kindergarten. The little girl in the following story is one of the girls that two years later got covered with ink when I dropped the ink bottle.

The year was about 1995. I had been married for over forty years and all my children were grown.

In the middle of the night I suddenly woke up with a start with my eyes wide open. I couldn't believe it. Moreover, I couldn't hide it any longer.

I reached over and shook my wife until she opened her eyes. If any of you have been married a long time you know that the first answer a wife gives when being awoken from a sound sleep, is "Not tonight, I'm too tired." I yelled at her, "Carole, Carole, I gotta tell ya, I gotta tell ya."

She finally said, "What?"

I said, "Carole, I made a promise in kindergarten over forty years ago and I can't keep that promise any longer." My wife looked at me like I was crazy.

I explained that in Number 11 School we had a sandbox in the kindergarten room and we all took turns playing in it, usually two at a time, and then it happened. My wife said, "Get to the point."

I told her when it happened we both ran out of the sandbox and hid among the other kids. The teacher came over to the sandbox and looked down and saw that it was wet and she asked, "WHO MADE SISSY IN THE SANDBOX?"

My wife said, "You did?"

"No, no, no, no, but Betty Smith made me promise that I would always keep it a secret that she was the one who made sissy in the sandbox."

My wife looked at me as if I had finally become a raging lunatic, rolled over and went back to sleep.

But I felt much better that I was finally able to tell the world who had done the horrible deed.

(In the year 2000 we held our high school class 50th reunion. I noticed on the attendance list that Betty Smith[1] is going to be there. I hope she forgives me for breaking my word and telling her secret. And if she asks, I'll again play in the sandbox with her if she has finally gotten all the black ink off of her from when I dropped the big ink bottle.)

The Dreaded Icebox

Certainly, refrigerators had been invented perhaps twenty to thirty years before I was born, however, my family and most families living in Passaic couldn't afford one. Also, the telephone had been invented many years before, however, we like most people in Passaic, simply couldn't afford a telephone in the 1930's.

But it wasn't the telephone that filled my heart with fear. It was the dreaded icebox.

*   *   *

What's an icebox? I was convinced that an icebox was invented by the devil to get children into enormous trouble. Let me explain.

An icebox normally has two compartments, a big compartment to put food into and a smaller compartment on the top. Every day the "ice man" would carry a large block of ice and put it into the top compartment.

The ice man, to get to our flat, would have to walk up the two flights of stairs carrying this heavy load of ice and squeeze it into the

---

1. Not her real name.

ice compartment and then securely close the door. As the ice melted, it cooled the food that was in the big compartment below the ice cabinet. Of course, each time you opened the door to the food compartment, two things happened. It would allow some of the room heat to go into the icebox which would cause the ice to melt faster. The second thing that would always happen would be my mother yelling at me, "You're melting the ice, close the icebox."

Because I knew she was going to yell at me I would always open and close the icebox as fast as I could. However, when you try to close the door too fast, it would slam and my mother would yell at me, "Don't ever slam the door of the icebox. You're going to make the ice move and melt faster." As I said, the icebox was invented by the devil, but this wasn't the worst part. The worst part occurred every afternoon when I came home from school.

My first job when I got home was to empty the water from the melted ice that collected in a large tray at the bottom of the ice compartment. This tray was only one inch tall but very wide and deep; about the size of a large tray that your mother used to bake cookies. And always the ice would melt so that the water was just below the top of the tray.

No matter how carefully I slid the tray out of the icebox, and no matter how slow and carefully I'd try to walk to the sink to empty it, always—and I mean always—some of the water would splash on the kitchen floor. My mother, who really loved me, would give me "great loves" each time this happened. These loves might include a lot of yelling, a good spanking, scolding, being sent to my room (as I previously described, I really did not have my own room, I shared it with my sister). Every afternoon as I left school I would run home but would slow down as the thought of emptying the water would come to mind. I knew that no matter how I did it I would find out how much my mother loved me that day.

The Day the Clock Stood Still

The Master Clock at Number 11 School was indeed an impressive mechanical wonder. It never stopped, not even in the great hurricane of 1938. But it did stop just after eleven a.m. on April 12, 1945.

It stopped at the exact minute that President Franklin Delano Roosevelt died.

And yet the first radio report of his death didn't occur for another forty minutes!

When the principal learned of the president's death he immediately called all the students into the auditorium. The principal then, in a very low voice, told us that the president had died—everyone started crying—the students, the teachers, and the principal. The principal said we should all pray for the soul of President Roosevelt and for divine guidance for our new president, Harry Truman. He then said we should all rush home and be with our families on this tragic day.

And we did. And it was indeed a tragic day.

When school started again several days later, all the clocks were still stuck at just after eleven a.m. But, miraculously after the Salute-to-the-Flag, and the teacher reading a psalm from the King James Bible followed by everyone reciting the 23rd Psalm from memory, the clocks again started working. Everyone at school thought it was a miracle.

*   *   *

I've often thought that the unexplained clock stoppage, and then starting just as we finished the 23rd Psalm should have been used to argue to the Supreme Court in favor of allowing prayers in school.

CHAPTER 4

My Friend Moishe

For my first sixteen years in Passaic, I lived in the Second Ward—the northern part of Passaic where the incinerator and the "Isolation Hospital" were located. My family lived just down the street from G. Directly across the street from G was where my good friend Moishe lived.

His real name was Morris but everyone that knew him called him Moishe. Moishe was much older than me (33 days and he never let me forget it). Although we were, and still are, great friends we also had a very competitive relationship. Let me give you just one example. We were ten years old and it was wintertime and the year was 1942. On the same property as our school was a red brick building which contained the Board of Education offices. The superintendent of Schools was Dr. Boone, whom we honored and feared like no other man in the entire world.

During that cold winter it snowed quite a bit. One day Moishe was walking on the sidewalk next to the school. He didn't see where I was hiding, although I was only twenty feet away waiting for him. I had made many large hard snowballs and had practiced my throwing. Knowing Moishe would soon walk by, I picked up an extra large snow ball. I was sure he didn't see me and as he walked just a little closer I wound up my pitching arm and threw the snowball at him full speed.

As soon as I released it I saw that walking behind Moishe was Dr. Boone. And even worse than that, I saw that Moishe had seen me and was about to duck, and he did duck under the snowball.

The snowball hit Dr. Boone squarely in the chest knocking him backwards. Moishe, being a man of honor and integrity immediately pointed at me and yelled, "Bobby threw the snowball, Bobby threw the snowball." Dr. Boone raced over and grabbed my arm. He marched me into the Board of Education building (from which, it was rumored, no student had ever escaped alive). He forced me to sit in the lobby and then told me my punishment was that I had to come and sit in that lobby for one hour every day for a month. As he said that I looked out the window and who was standing there with a big smile on his face? My friend Moishe!

These adventures with Moishe continued every day throughout our childhood.

*   *   *

Moishe and I were part of a group of Jewish boys who went to public school for the full day; it ended at 2:45 p.m. Then every day we raced across Monroe Street to the Tulip Street Hebrew School which started at 3:00 and ended at 5:30 p.m. We started going to Hebrew School at age 6 and continued to about age 15. We were very sheltered and really knew almost nothing about Christianity. In fact, it wasn't until I was ten years old that I first learned that Jesus Christ was the founder and Messiah of all Christianity.

However, don't get the wrong impression. My classmates weren't saints. We all knew how to curse. But, of course, we didn't know what the various cuss words meant.

Let me give you an example of Moishe's and my naivete. We were about eight years old, two years before we learned about Christianity, and had returned early to Number 11 School from lunch.

We were walking on the first floor, on the west side of our school. Off that hall, among other things, there was the nature study room which had a large greenhouse attached to it. The nature study teacher was Mrs.

McKonky. She was a large woman who had a very strange body build. Instead of where women usually bulge out in front, she bulged out much lower (later in life I learned that this occurs on women who do not wear bras) but we didn't understand it at that time. We always just considered her some sort of a freak of nature.

As we walked through the hall Moishe and I got into some kind of an argument (as we always did) and Moishe said very loudly, "Jesus Christ, Bobby, you're wrong again."

At that very instant Mrs. McKonky grabbed us by the back of our shirts and spun us around and sternly said, "Never use the Lord's name in vain." Of course we were frightened (remember the coffin that was in the lobby) and we promised her we would never do it again.

After she walked away I said, "Moishe, I never knew that the Lord's name was 'Bobby.'"

The Spitball Affair

The clock continues to tick very slowly. I sit at my cramped desk (I was now eleven years old and still sitting in the desk I used when I was six) not paying any attention, just simply carving my initials in my desk top with my pocket knife. Across from me, Moishe is daydreaming and playing with some paper. I decided, as usual, to totally ignore him.

It is now 4:05 p.m. The year is 1943. We are in the Tulip Street Hebrew School. Our teacher, Mr. Witte, is in front of the room attempting to teach us something. What it is I'll never understand.

Everyone in our Hebrew class loves, hates, adores, worships, reveres, enjoys and detests Mr. Witte. He is from the "old school of teaching." Mr. Witte loves all of his students, and the way you show love in the "old school of teaching," is by hitting the students.

I don't mean just hitting. I mean using a hammer handle to hit the students. I don't really mean just using a hammer handle, a metal B-X cable is perhaps his most potent weapon.

Of course, we don't like to be hit, but we really knew he was showing us love. (Maybe he is preparing us for marriage later on.)

Of course, some of the kids in the class get hit more often than others. Some never get hit, particularly those that look like "angels." Damn it, Moishe always looks like an angel; small, sweet-looking with the aura of innocence in his eyes.

Unfortunately, it is obvious that I don't look like an angel because I receive more than my share of "love" from Mr. Witte. But today this isn't on my mind. I am simply minding my own business, being good, and just carving my initials in the desk.

Out of the corner of my eye I see the angel, Moishe, slowly taking a piece of paper, rolling it into a ball and then putting it in his mouth and slowly chewing on this ball of paper. I figure, maybe angels have part billy goat in them. I go back to carving my desk.

Then I notice that Moishe has transformed the paper he was chewing into a hard rolled up ball, the size of a good marble. He then carefully aims it at Mr. Witte, whose back is turned to the class as he writes on the blackboard.

Moishe's thumb flicks, off flies the speeding spitball. The trajectory is perfect; it strikes Mr. Witte on the back of the neck.

Time stands still as Mr. Witte turns around. Everyone in the class turns to look at Moishe. Mr. Witte reaches into his desk, takes out the dreaded hammer handle, and storms up the aisle. About half way up the aisle, Moishe, the angel, turns on his brightest smile and points his forefinger across the aisle at—you know it and I know it—it was at me!!

Mr. Witte reaches me and begins to hit me on the back with the hammer handle. There never is a good time to be hit with a hammer handle; but this was worse than most times. I was just being good, carving my desk. So in my surprise, shock and outrage I scream out, "JESUS CHRIST! Why are you hitting me?"

As soon as I said it, I knew that was a horrible mistake. Using the name "Jesus Christ" to an ultra-religious Jew is always very risky. To shout out the name "JESUS CHRIST!" to an Orthodox Jew who has a hammer handle over your head is not only risky, it's downright stupid. Mr. Witte again starts pounding me with the hammer handle, pounds me and pounds me; more love and more love.

Finally gaining composure I apologize by saying, "Jesus, Mr. Witte, I'm sorry," Oh my God, I did it again!

As I try to protect my head by putting it in my arms, I sneak a peak across the aisle towards Moishe.

There he is; serene, looking like an angel.

That's My Friend Moishe.

CHAPTER 5

The War Years

Walking to Broadway

Broadway in Passaic is a wonderfully wide boulevard with stores on both sides.

To get to upper Broadway from my "flat" you walked down the hill toward Moishe's house and turned left on Paulison Avenue. The walk would then take you past where many of my friends lived. For example, when you walked past Second Ward Park, Charlie and Jerry Siegel lived in the apartment house. In many ways I was always jealous of these twin brothers. They were good students with good penmanship who were always on the winning spelling bee's team. In fact, I used to give them the worst insult I knew, "You're so smart, you might as well be girls."

Paulison Avenue intersects Broadway three blocks past the park. On the far corner was another apartment house where a friend of mine, Julian Kivowitz, lived. He was also one of those guys that always studied. On the near corner was a large apartment house where my aunt and uncle lived.

I truly believed that my aunt and uncle's apartment house was incredibly luxurious. It had a beautiful lobby and an elegant elevator. They didn't have to shovel the coal to get heat; heat was provided to them. Yes, it was true luxury.

On a Sunday in early December 1941, I went with my parents to my aunt and uncle's apartment for a large family party. There were lots of people in their apartment including my cousin, Marilyn, who was my same age and in my class at Number 11 School.

Suddenly somebody yelled, "QUIET!" The apartment got totally quiet and the radio had been turned up. We then all heard the announcement that, "The Japanese have just attacked Pearl Harbor." Everybody in the room was shocked, because it was obvious that America was now at war with Japan. Some of the women began to cry because when there is a war, young men have to fight in it and young men die in a war.

But within a few minutes the shock and worry turned into outright anger. People were incensed about this Japanese sneak attack that had apparently killed thousands of Americans in Hawaii. Some of the men said they were going to go volunteer and join the Army. Over the next few days, tens of thousands of Americans stood in line, not only in Passaic, but throughout the country to join the Army.

Of course I was only nine and couldn't join the Army, but by 1942 everybody, including my classmates, were involved in efforts to help win the war. Young men 18 to about 35 were either volunteering or being drafted into the Army. Those that were too old or were "4F" (i.e. physically unfit to be in the military like my father) volunteered for other crucial assignments. Even children had crucial war assignments.

For example, my father became an air raid warden. He was given some training, a white steel helmet and a flashlight. His job was, if there would be an air-raid, to stand outside and make sure there were no lights on that would help the enemy bombers find the city of Passaic. And everyone assumed that Passaic would be a prime target for the Germans to bomb because of its heavy industrialization. Our city had many factories making rubber goods for both the Army and the Navy. The city also had a large number of companies that made electrical equipment for the military. Thus, we really believed that Passaic would be a major target that enemy bombers would aim for.

To get ready before any bombers would arrive, the city would periodically have air-raid drills. These drills would involve having the sirens go off; sirens had been hastily mounted on telephone poles throughout the city. When you heard the siren, you had to immediately scurry inside the nearest building. If you were in a car, you stopped the car and ran into the nearest building. If the drill was at night, you had to shut off all the lights or you put black curtains over the windows. The air raid wardens had the dangerous job of being outside and enforcing this blackout. I was indeed very proud of my father being an air raid warden.

The war effort consumed everyone. My mother, like most women in Passaic, volunteered for various duties during the war. For example, she knitted scarfs and sweaters for our servicemen. Every afternoon she would go to the American Red Cross Headquarters on Passaic Avenue and roll bandages. She also worked very hard selling war bonds—the government needed a lot of money to fight the war, and the way they convinced people to buy bonds is they offered them $4, after ten years, for every $3 that they would invest. To help War Bond sales, the city built a tiny building in a parking space in front of W.T. Grant Five and Dime Store on Lexington Avenue in downtown Passaic. The little building was only about ten feet long, five feet wide and eight feet high. Different volunteers sat in the building all day long with the window open selling War Bonds. If people didn't have that much money, then they could buy "War Stamps" in amounts as small as ten cents. My mother was one of those volunteers.

All of us in school were also very active in helping the war effort. For example, used newspaper was in need to help win the war, and the War Department asked the children of America to collect old newspapers and turn them in at the schools. My friend Moishe and I went to everybody in the local neighborhood and collected their newspapers which we temporarily stored in the basement of my house. Every other Friday we would bring the newspapers that we had collected to the school.

We were very successful in collecting newspapers, in fact, so successful that my basement began to get full of newspaper. The pile of papers kept creeping closer and closer to the coal burning furnace that provided heat for the "flat."

One day the city's fire marshall came to my house and walked into the basement and almost fainted. He made me go out and find my friends to immediately remove all newspapers from within 20 feet of the furnace. Since we had to still store the papers until the next Friday, we put the newspapers all over the wooden steps that led to our second floor "flat." We did leave a skinny little space so my parents could squeeze up the stairs. None of us ever considered the possibility that if the papers would catch fire on the wooden steps no one would be able to get out of the house. We were too concerned about helping win the war.

Finally it was Friday and my school would accept all the newspapers. I had so many newspapers that Moishe and I had to go back and forth and back and forth using my Red Flyer wagon filled with newspapers to take them to school. Moishe and I loaded the wagon very high and my mother helped push the wagon the three blocks to the school. As I remember it took hundreds of trips to the school, but it was probably only about ten trips.

When you took the newspapers to school they would weigh them and write down how many each person brought in. Perhaps the proudest thing that ever happened to me during World War II is that I collected the most newspapers in my entire school. I was awarded the "General Eisenhower Paper Collection Award." It was a bright medal on a red, white and blue ribbon. (Today I still have and cherish that medal.)

And this was just part of the war effort.

President Roosevelt issued a special request asking boys my age to help protect American cities from German and Japanese bombers. He requested—and of course a request by this great president was the same as a command—that we should build scale models of both the enemy and American airplanes. Each model was to be approximately one foot across the wing span and to have two hooks on top of it—one forward and one aft—the models were to be painted dull black The purpose of the models was to train anti-aircraft gunners and the air-raid wardens on how to recognize the difference between enemy planes and American airplanes.

To train the anti-aircraft gunners and air raid wardens, they tied a wire across a darkened room. The wire would start about eight feet off the ground and on the opposite wall it would be about three feet off the ground. A model airplane would then be hooked to the high end of the wire in the darkened room. The airplane, which was painted black, was difficult to see. One after another the airplanes would rapidly slide down the wire and the aircraft gunners and the air raid wardens would shout out what kind of airplanes they were: German Junker bomber, Japanese Zero, American B-17, British Spitfire, etc.

All of us kids feverishly worked building the models. We all helped each other so that the models would be perfect replicas of the various war planes. I, unfortunately, was the worst model maker of the entire group. However, my friend Moishe was the best model maker (and he didn't ever let me forget it). Together we built quite good model airplanes.

Because of the war, getting balsa wood for the models was very difficult. However, we found that we could substitute soft southern pine even though it was harder to whittle with a knife. There was also a great shortage of paint so we invented various ways to modify the black ink from school into paint. We "borrowed" the big ink bottles from the school and mixed the ink with water to make paint. (By the way, none of my friends ever allowed me to carry one of the big ink bottles.)

As a reward, after our group finished our one hundredth airplane, the military invited three of the model makers to visit the U.S. Army's anti-aircraft defense site that was located no more than four blocks from my house—on the empty hill behind the city incinerator. The Army had installed five anti-aircraft guns and built barracks so that the soldiers could sleep there. (I was invited probably because of my father's effort as an air raid warden. Moishe did not get an invitation which of course, I gloated about).

The night we were invited to go see these anti-aircraft guns, they were doing a training session inside of their barracks. We watched them put up the wire in the room and then watched our models— models made with our own hands—sliding down the wire and all the Army gunners yelling out what kind of airplane it was. The captain in charge gave us boys the job of correcting the gunners if they yelled out the wrong name. We were very proud that we were helping win the war.

This practice continued for about one half hour and then they served us refreshments. Just as the cookies were being passed around, the air-raid sirens went off. We didn't know, and neither did the air-craft gunners know, if it was a real air-raid or just another air-raid drill.

The gunners ran out from the building, first shutting off all of the lights. When they reached their guns they began tilting them up towards the sky and started loading ammunition. While all this was going on, my friends and I were peeking out the door. We couldn't go out because the Army had stationed an "M.P." (Military Policeman) at the door. However, since we were on a hill which was the highest point in the city of Passaic, we could look down and see all the house lights being turned off. Then the giant search lights were turned on, shining their beams into the sky looking for airplanes. The soldiers had their helmets on. I tried to see where I lived and I imagined I saw my father, with his white helmet on, walking with his flashlight. Suddenly somebody outside yelled, "There's a German Junker Bomber" and all the aircraft guns began to turn and one of them began to fire tracer bullets into the sky. As soon as that gun started firing, they all started firing. My friends and I were really scared. We were under a real air-raid attack and were right where the gunners were. The noise from the guns was incredible.

The guns fired for only a few minutes and then someone yelled, "CEASE FIRE." We wondered, did they shoot down the German airplane?

Well, to make this long story much shorter, they didn't shoot down any German airplanes. In fact there were no German airplanes in the sky over the city of Passaic, that night nor any night. In fact, there were never any German airplanes anywhere over the United States throughout the war.

Someone had apparently seen an American airplane and yelled out it was the German Junker Bomber, and because of that, everybody started shooting. It was all a big mistake.

However, when you shoot explosive shells into the air, just like when you throw a ball high in the air, sooner or later it will fall down and hit the ground. And so it happened all over the northern part of the city of Passaic. The shells from the aircraft guns began falling back on the city causing some fires. The Passaic Fire Department—which by the way was the first mechanized fire department east of the Mississippi River—raced around town and the air-raid wardens were running with their small water pumps to help fight some of the fires.

It was a little bit of a miracle that nobody got hurt and the damage was small, but it taught my friends and me how important it was that these anti-aircraft gunners, airplane lookouts and air-raid wardens be better trained using our models.

And so when we got back home we began building more and more models. In fact, over the four years of the war, Moishe and I built almost 200 different models which we gave to our air defense people. It didn't surprise us, after all that effort, that America won the war in 1945.

*   *   *

The firing of the anti-aircraft guns was immediately classified as a WAR SECRET by the Army officer in charge of the Passaic Defense Battalion. Before we three model makers were allowed to leave the Army barracks they swore us to secrecy. They said if we ever told anyone about the guns firing, it would help Germany win the war. Also, they said if we told anyone we would be traitors and could be shot or sent to Leavenworth Prison.

The Army also told this to the Herald News reporter who was sent to investigate the story of a German air raid. The reporter was then told it was a WAR SECRET and the newspaper could not print any story. And they didn't.

The next day at school, Moishe ignored me. He did not want to give me the chance to brag about visiting the anti-aircraft guns. Thus, I never told him or anyone else the WAR SECRET.

CHAPTER 6

Passaic Highlights

Second Ward Park

Directly adjacent to Number 11 School was a beautiful tree laden park with multiple flower beds. The trees—majestic elms—were laid out in a stately double row through the center of the park directly aimed at the impressive front door of the school. The elm trees provided shade over numerous park benches, thereby causing cool breezes in the hot and humid New Jersey summers. On the northern side of the shade trees were baseball and football fields. They were well kept and modern facilities. On the southern side of the shade trees was a series of lovely curved walkways that led to and around circular flower beds that were planted with many different varieties. Intermingled in this side of the park were additional shade trees and other concrete supported wooden benches.

Unfortunately, when I last visited the park—the first time after being away from Passaic for forty years—my heart was truly broken. Apparently Dutch Elm Disease had killed all the trees and now there was just an open unattractive landscape with a few scraggily trees. However, in my mind it will always be beautiful like when I was a young child.

*　　　　　*　　　　　*

One of my earliest recollections occurred prior to me going to public school. I must have been four years old. I didn't realize it but the entire world, including the United States (and in particular, Passaic) was deep into the national economic depression. There wasn't even money for food.

However, somehow the city of Passaic managed to have enough funds to come to the park each afternoon and give the children a pint of milk and some graham crackers. Although initially I remember my mother being very hesitant for me to go to the park at that time ("We don't want people to think we are on 'relief'"), I did convince her to let me go to the park every day in the summertime.

Usually three city trucks arrived at about 2:00 p.m. The first truck had milk and cookies which we all waited in line and eagerly obtained, drank and ate. While this was going on the other two trucks were setting up a portable movie screen. I don't know how large the screen was but I remember thinking it was gigantic. I would think it was at least twenty feet high by thirty feet wide. After the screen was erected the "projector truck" drove around and got into position and started testing the movie projector. Then they waited and we waited for it to get dark.

Everyone went home for dinner. Following dinner everybody returned to the park for that evening's movie. All of these movies were old silent pictures which none of us kids had ever seen before. In fact, we had never seen "non-talkies" before. Thus, we thought this was a great new kind of entertainment.

Researchers show that one of the great memories people have is of aromas. If your mother wore a particular brand of perfume, for the rest of your life whenever you smelled that brand, you would think of your mother. Well, the same was true for going to the movies in the park because everybody wore citronella—a very sweet smelling mosquito repellent. And citronella was a life-saver from the dreaded "New Jersey mosquito."

New Jersey was famous for its giant mosquitoes which truly sucked the blood out of everybody. The mosquitoes came from the swamps that were between Secaucus and Passaic (only in the 1980's did they begin calling swamps "wetlands"). Even with the citronella, the mosquito biting was fierce. However, we always sat through the entire so-called silent movie cheering the hero and booing the villain.

When the Second World War ended in 1945, the U.S. Army donated its surplus DDT to various cities including Passaic. The DDT was spread extensively through the "swamp" area and was very effective in killing off these gigantic mosquitoes, causing the sweet smell of citronella to disappear from Second Ward Park.

*   *   *

On the northern edge of Second Ward Park was Paulison Avenue. If you turned right on Paulison and walked one block you would be at the start of a large hill (the "Isolation Hospital" and the city's incinerator were at the very top). The reason that's important is there used to be a major creek that flowed down from that hill. However, the creek had been covered and the creek water routed via concrete pipes. Unfortunately, the concrete pipes were too small.

What this meant was that the pipe worked extremely well when the weather was dry. However, when you have a major storm, the pipe was unable to handle the volume and Second Ward Park, which was an oval approximately eight feet deep and about 700 feet on each side, began to fill up with water. In fact, it would fill up totally with water in a hurricane. Thus, instead of having a park you would have an eight foot muddy dangerous pool.

The impact of our park being this potential swamp or muddy pool was very interesting. We kids, as we grew older, realized that the richer part of Passaic—Third Ward—had tennis courts, and all those rich kids played tennis. We had no tennis courts in Second Ward. Why? Because the city said with the occasional flooding, they could not keep the tennis courts in any type of reasonable condition.

Finally after a really horrible storm, where the park not only filled but overflowed into people's houses, the city finally decided to fix the drainage problem in Second Ward Park. Giant new concrete pipes were installed, and when it was completed, the flooding was only a memory. Even better, we not only got three new tennis courts, but also permanent grandstands for the baseball diamond. However, the tennis courts arrived too late for many of us to learn and become proficient. Therefore, these damn rich kids in Third Ward always dominated the Passaic tennis teams.

Mischief Night

Passaic was the great melting pot. As previously described, the city was basically populated by the families of first generation adults who had been born in America. It was a city of opportunity. However, it was a city that still had its memories and roots in the old countries.

There were pockets of "small ghettos" scattered throughout the city. These pockets were either totally Polish, or Hungarian, or Jews from Eastern Europe, or Italians, or what we called in those days, Negroes. And Second Ward Park was right in the middle of a major group of these ghettos.

Amazingly, the kids from all these different ghettos got along fairly well. They were tolerant of each other and there were very few major fights except for "Mischief Night."

The night before Halloween, in Passaic, was called Mischief Night. That was the night that you would take candles and wax up people's windows or ring doorbells or do other kinds of minor vandalism. It was not like the modern Halloween. You didn't say Trick or Treat because there were no treats. Passaic was still in an economic depression. Thus, there were only tricks. And there was the much anticipated "yearly fight."

On Mischief Night, as it began to get dark, the kids from various pockets of ethnic culture wandered down to Second Ward Park. Somehow they knew to separate into different groups by age in different areas of the park, and when it was totally dark pushing and shoving broke out. Sure, the cops knew about it, and sure they always came with their sirens blazing, and of course, everybody ran away when that occurred. That was part of Mischief Night. It was fun to almost get into a fight knowing, just like in the western movies, the cavalry would save you—the police cars' flashing lights would save you. So even I, the coward of all cowards, used to go to Second Ward Park on Mischief Night. Admittedly, I always hid behind a tree, but I could say that I was one of the warriors.

Second Ward Park was the place to be. There were always many pickup baseball or football games going on in the park. There was always fun. It was the center of activity for all Second Warders. It was beautiful and wonderful. Although I'm not an emotional person, when I went back to see it forty years later when the landscape was denuded and there wasn't any beauty left, I truly cried for its past greatness. If I have one wish for the city of Passaic, that wish is to replant the trees and let the park again be the great hope for the minorities, the meeting point and the melting pot that it was intended to be.

Passaic "Wonder Teams"

Throughout my youth I kept hearing about Passaic's previous "Wonder Teams." These teams compiled the greatest high school basketball record that there ever was! Today, more than eighty years later, the Passaic Wonder Teams' incredible accomplishments are still included in the "Guinness Book of World Records."

Under the direction of Ernest "Professor" Blood, the basketball teams had achieved 159 consecutive victories, an unprecedented record covering six years, from December 17, 1919 and ending February 6, 1925.

Both Passaic's Wonder Team and Coach Blood were subsequently elected into the Basketball Hall of Fame.

"The victories accumulated during their winning period were not only from playing high school teams. There were wins over prep schools and college freshman squads, such as Newark College and Philadelphia All-Scholastics. And every time there was a victory for these Wonder Teams, a factory whistle would sound two long blasts; one blast was heard for defeat.

"After the 147th victory and many straight state titles, Blood moved on. Twelve games later, the 'Boys from the Hill' accepted defeat as Hackensack High broke their winning streak. That night in Passaic, only one long blast echoed throughout the city, signaling more than defeat...marking the end of an era."

Textile Mills

Equaling the Wonder Team was the pride Passaic had in their giant textile mills, both in the city and in the surrounding towns along the Passaic River. These included the Botany Mills, the Forstmann Mills that produced woolen fabrics, the Gary Mills and others. These mills produced much of the textiles for the entire United States. During my youth in the 1940's they were still growing and it seemed they would be there forever.

No one realized that in less than a decade all of these mills would be out of business. They would have closed their doors, laid off all their employees and moved to the southern parts of the United States to get rid of the high wages obtained by the aggressive Passaic labor unions that flourished in Passaic. But before that happened, the textile mills brought great prosperity.

For example, Julius Forstmann, the president of Forstmann Mills, built a beautiful stone library for the city of Passaic which is still there today, more than seventy years from when it first opened. But Passaic wasn't only textiles and a basketball team, it was also the birthplace of America's electronic technological revolution.

The Magic Radio

As I had mentioned, my father, along with his brother, owned a men's store on Monroe Street on the corner of Lucille Place. This was just two blocks from Number 11 school. On the occasional days when I didn't go to Hebrew School, I would sometimes walk to my father's store. His store was one of four stores that occupied the first floor of a four story walk-up apartment house.

One of those stores was empty in early 1938, but it had a new sign in the window. It stated that the store would be open for three hours a day next week for people to see a new invention and they could make comments on what they thought of it. In order to get into the store to see the invention's demonstration, each person needed a special entrance ticket.

Luckily, because my father's store was so near this planned demonstration, he was given several tickets and proudly gave me one of the tickets.

The store was to open fifteen minutes after school closed. I decided to skip Hebrew School and ran from Number 11 School to be there on time. I managed to get in line before the door opened. When the door opened the whole store was empty except for something that looked like a large radio receiver. There were obviously speakers mounted in it and a dial on the outside that looked different from a normal radio dial. It, of course, like all good radios in that day, was made out of wood. However, in the very center of this "radio receiver" was a piece of glass about four inches in diameter.

After about fifteen minutes, the place was quite full and at that moment several hosts gave everybody pencils and forms that were sealed. They asked that none of us open the forms until after the demonstration started.

Then like magic the glass window in this big radio set began to light up and we couldn't believe what we saw. In the middle of the glass window was a Felix the Cat doll sitting on a bar stool. The picture was a little fuzzy, but there was no question—it was Felix the Cat, the star of an extremely popular comic strip. As we watched the doll sitting on the stool, the host told us that this picture was being transmitted through the air from Passaic's Third Ward (just off Main Avenue and Brook Street) from the Alan B. DuMont Laboratories. Moreover, the host was telling us that this picture was being received at eight different stores located throughout Passaic.

To say the least, everybody in the room was astounded by this miracle of having a picture appear on the screen that had been transmitted for several miles.

The commentator then asked us to open up the questionnaire and start filling in the form. At that instant, Felix was moved and was now lying down on the seat. The crowd in the store felt that was even more astounding because it showed that you could do moving pictures this way.

There were a number of questions on how clear you thought the picture was and could you make out what was the model in the picture, etc. Perhaps the most interesting question was what do you think this new invention should be named. I immediately wrote down the first thing that came to my mind "Picture Radio." The questionnaire then asked you to put down a second choice and I put down "Radio View." I noticed people in the audience were writing down other names. After about fifteen minutes the picture disappeared and the moderator thanked everyone and they collected the forms.

*   *   *

The following year, RCA (now part of General Electric) astounded the world by introducing "television" to the world at the 1939 New York Worlds Fair. They didn't tell anyone that the heart of the television—the Cathode Ray Picture Tube—had been invented and built in Passaic by Dr. Alan B. DuMont.

*   *   *

Television disappeared and then reappeared after the Second World War. Then the Alan B. DuMont Laboratories in Passaic produced large quantities of the DuMont television sets. Yes, there were other competitive brands starting production at that time, but none had the prestige or the quality of the DuMont television sets.

In addition, DuMont also started a television channel, which still exists today as Channel 5 in New York City.

However, unfortunately for Passaic, this major advance in technology by the DuMont Laboratories was short lived. Others with much greater capital resources (e.g. RCA, GE, Admiral, Motorola) took over the television industry and finally the Alan B. DuMont Company went out of business. It was indeed a sad day for Passaic.

Trains and Trolleys

In the booming 1920's and even in the depression 1930's, downtown Passaic was the great shopping hub for a good part of northern New Jersey. Main Street was lined with banks and prestige stores. On Lexington Avenue, which was parallel to Main Street, there were even more stores, including several department stores and three gigantic "five and dime" stores. Separating these two major streets were the infamous Erie Railroad Tracks.

The Erie Railroad provided frequent passenger service from New York City to Passaic, Paterson and even beyond. To be technical, the Erie Railroad didn't really come from New York City. The trains started in

Jersey City, New Jersey, which is next to the Hudson River. The railroad provided a free ferry boat ride from New York's Chambers Street to the train in Jersey City.

The typical train had approximately ten passenger cars as well as a mail car. They were all powered by powerful steam locomotives.

The trains crossed the Passaic River near Passaic Park and then entered downtown Passaic at a rather high speed on a highly banked turn at State Street, near the Salvation Army building and the YMCA. (In my first year of engineering school, we studied "America's Engineering Marvels." I was astonished, but very proud, to discover that Passaic's State Street high banked speed railroad track was listed in the Top 100 Engineering Marvels.)

After the high speed turn, the trains would start to slow down. They then proceeded on a straight track between Lexington and Main Avenues. The railroad's single stop in Passaic was directly across from the city's only skyscraper, which my generation called the "People's Bank Building." People now call it "555 Main Avenue."

The train station had the ticket office and waiting room on the side of the track near Lexington Avenue. Because it was dangerous to walk across the railroad tracks, there was a passenger underground tunnel that took you under the tracks so you could board the trains heading to New York City.

I had many cousins who lived in New York City, so almost every Saturday my mother and I took the train, then the ferry boat, then the New York subways to the Bronx to visit my cousins. Occasionally, my cousins came to Passaic. When they did we would almost always walk to "downtown" and look at the stores on Main Street and watch the steam locomotive trains arrive and depart.

My New York cousins always ridiculed Passaic because it didn't have a "subway." Finally, I discovered the perfect answer to their ridicule. The next time my cousins visited, I forced them to go to the Erie Railroad's ticket office and pointed with pride at the sign that said, "Use Subway to go to East Bound Track." I then marched them out to show them our subway—a thirty foot long pedestrian tunnel about fifteen feet under ground. My cousins acted like they weren't impressed. But they never again ridiculed Passaic.

*   *   *

Main Avenue was the major thoroughfare that connected Paterson, New Jersey, in one direction with Newark, New Jersey, in the other direction. Between Paterson, Passaic and Newark, there was of course, the city of Clifton that almost surrounded Passaic as well as many other small towns.

The Passaic trolley cars, run by the electric company, were one of the most modern trolleys in America, and they were enormous fun to ride. However, Passaic, like almost every other city in America, succumbed to the auto industry's propaganda that having trolleys was old fashioned, hurt a city's image, and caused traffic congestion. Thus, in 1939, Passaic's trolley cars stopped running, and their tracks were removed from Main Avenue.

It was interesting that almost thirty years later General Motors Corporation and a major rubber tire company were convicted of anti-trust charges for coercing cities into ending trolley service. Even though this was perhaps one of the greatest harms done to the cities in the twentieth century, the penalty that General Motors and the rubber company received was insignificant. In fact, if my memory serves me right, it was only a $1 fine for each company.

Replacing the trolley cars were electric buses (of course built by General Motors). Each bus had a large "trapeze" attached to its roof, which "rubbed" off the overhead electric lines that had previously run the trolleys.

The argument to switch to buses was that they were maneuverable and could go through traffic where the trolley cars were on fixed rails, and therefore, only blocked traffic. That argument had logic, however, like many things that logic was totally false.

Shortly after the Second World War, the use of electrically operated buses ended. The bus companies all bought new diesel burning, polluting buses (obviously, also made by General Motors).

So Passaic "advanced" from a non-pollution public transportation system using trolleys, that everybody enjoyed riding and were extremely low cost to operate. In its place, the city ended up with polluting buses that were ten times more expensive than trolleys and that blocked the streets more and provided much inferior transportation.

Yes, it was (and is) a blunder of historic proportions.

*   *   *

It was always fun to be downtown when an Erie train roared in and stopped at the station. There were crossings of the railroad tracks at five different streets (State Street, Passaic Avenue, Broadway, Jefferson Street and Monroe Street). During the 1930's, at each of these crossings there was a man lowering gates to block the pedestrians and cars from crossing the tracks. These gate operators sat in little houses to protect themselves from the weather. When the bell went off in the house, they would go out with a hand crank and lower the gates.

Obviously, this tied up all the traffic trying to go across the city.

After the war, there was a great advance made by the Erie Railroad in Passaic. They installed automatic gates for the manual gates. This occurred at the same time that automatic traffic lights were installed. Prior to this a policeman at each crossing manually operated the traffic lights to smooth out the traffic flow.

As always seems to happen, when a "modernization" is made (such as installing automatic gates at the train cross streets and automatic traffic lights), it created newer, bigger traffic jams than ever.

*   *   *

Arguably, the greatest invention the British ever made was the steam locomotive. It was indeed the marvel of the 19th century.

The most impressive time of any steam locomotive is when it starts from a standing still position with a full load of cars behind it. It belches smoke and starts slowly with a "chew—chew—chew" and it finally speeds up to where it goes "chew-chew-chew." However, unfortunately, Passaic happened to be in the exact range when the initial coal that they used in the locomotive to make steam had to be replenished. Thus, while the train sat in the Passaic station unloading and loading passengers, the fireman shoveled coal into the boiler. The consequence of this was that when the train first started lugging itself forward—chew—chew—chew—it would be belching black smoke which would be full of coal cinders. They would get everything in downtown Passaic filthy—the store fronts, the cars, and people's hair.

Passaic was famous for the trains running down the middle of the main street. Yet everyone complained about them. In response, the city government constantly tried to convince the Erie Railroad to end their train service, even though it was profitable and a needed service so that people could commute, at low cost, to Paterson or New York City. Erie Railroad ignored these pleas until after World War II.

In the late 1940's and through the 1950's, all railroads in the U.S. deliberately downgraded their passenger business to concentrate on freight transportation where they believed there was more money to be made. What this short-sighted business strategy meant was that they no longer invested any money in upgrading the passenger cars or the train stations. In a short period of time, the trains became disgustingly dirty, the stations were run down, and passengers began shifting to either using cars or the more expensive inter-city bus services.

The Erie Railroad finally got what it wanted. The government regulators agreed that they could end passenger service to their "Main Line"—i.e. ending passenger service to Passaic and Paterson. A short time later, in order to save the Erie Railroad from bankruptcy, it was forced to merge with the Lackawanna Railroad; a railroad that still carried passengers using its Passaic Park Station.

It was ironic that Passaic's passenger trains no longer went downtown where working people needed low cost transportation to jobs in New York and Paterson. Instead it stopped in the richer part of the city, Passaic Park, predominantly servicing passengers that were "Yuppies" working on Wall Street.

When the Erie Railroad ended its downtown train service, Passaic was given a once in a lifetime chance to enhance the downtown area. Suddenly the railroad right-of-way that split the city in half was being dismantled. The tracks were torn up and the more than fifty foot wide roadway ended up as a gift to the city.

And what did the city do with this once in a lifetime opportunity? They turned this most valuable property, which many people thought could revolutionize Passaic, into a huge parking lot to support the somewhat old and somewhat obsolete stores along Main and Lexington Avenue. These stores were being challenged by new types of shopping; first, by the revolutionary strip shopping centers on highways, and then by the giant shopping malls many miles from Passaic.

But the passing years have proved that Passaic probably made the correct choice by building the huge parking area. It is now more than thirty years since they built this new parking area in Passaic, and unlike most older cities, the downtown has not only survived, it has flourished against all the new shopping centers.

Yes, there have been many advances and changes in Passaic since I grew up, but perhaps the one thing that I missed the most is the wonderful sound of steam locomotives pulling the passenger trains through downtown Passaic. To illustrate how much that memory means to me, for my 65th birthday my entire family treated me to what they called the "Passaic History Holiday." We went to Strasburg,

Pennsylvania, where they still run steam locomotives between the City of Strasburg and the City of Paradise. As our train approached the City of Paradise and the steam whistle sounded, it reminded me of my youth in paradise—i.e., the City of Passaic, New Jersey.

PART 2

High School

The Greatest Years

CHAPTER 7

From Number 11 School to Passaic High

By June of 1947, the war had been over for almost two years, and the post war economic boom was just being recognized. People were no longer frightened that there would be another great depression. People were spending money at a record rate; money that they had saved during the war.

The anti-aircraft batteries had been totally removed from North Passaic and a building boom was under way, similar to Levittown in Long Island, New York, and Pennsylvania. The entire hills of North Passaic were suddenly covered by new small single family homes. In less than a year and a half hundreds of new homes had been built in the barren wasteland next to the incinerator.

In that June my class graduated from Number 11 Junior High School. Many of the parents and grandparents that attended the graduation had never themselves gone beyond seventh grade on their own. Thus, watching their children reach the major milestone of completing grade nine was a source of great joy and honor.

The graduation took place in the wonderful auditorium in Number 11 school. It was packed with the relatives.

The graduation ceremony was deliberately quite formal. We marched in to the music teacher playing Pomp and Circumstance on the piano.

We had been drilled and drilled on marching slowly and keeping our faces stern and "grin free." Even my friend Moishe accomplished this.

During the ceremony the class sang many songs. Perhaps the most memorable song for the audience was Shenandoah. However, the song that I'll remember best is the one in which my friend Moishe had the solo singing part. It was a song about a Boll Weevil in cotton. Since I always considered my friend Moishe to be a weevil (or is it a "weasel")—at times an unwanted pest—I thought it was appropriate that he sang the solo. But I must admit he truly did have a voice like an angel even though he was still the shortest guy in the class. However, I was the second shortest and I could see that he was starting to grow, and obviously I was envious of him even more.

The highlight of graduation came when Mr. Cruise gave each graduate a diploma and a copy of the United States Constitution. Their relatives roared, cheered and many cried.

The graduation ceremony ended in late afternoon and we marched off the stage with everybody waving their diploma to the tune of Pomp and Circumstance again being beaten forth from the piano.

Parents rushed and hugged their kids. My grandfather, an immigrant from eastern Russia, like many immigrants in America, had started night school when he arrived in our country in 1900 from eastern Russia. By 1947 he had spent 47 years in night school and had already graduated from ninth grade. He was well on his way towards his high school diploma. However, he was very proud of both my cousin and classmate, Marilyn, and me, and he truly believed that graduating from junior high was just the first of many steps we would take.

Although all the parents wanted their kids to go out with them to celebrate, there was a secret party planned by one of the graduates who lived on Howe Avenue. He had somehow arranged for his parents to be away on this monumental day, and therefore, he invited everyone to come to the secret party. And just about everybody did come.

I'm not sure how many there were in the graduating class, but there were at least 100 and probably more at this party. As classmates continued to arrive at the house, it became more and more crowded.

This was the first time I'd ever been to a party with both boys and girls without adults. All my friends swaggered at this great opportunity. However, they were all, just like me, scared to death about what to do or how to talk to the girls.

The party turned out just like the school's chaperoned dances had turned out—the boys stayed on one side of the room, and the girls on the other side, without either group talking to the other. That is the way it remained until my classmate, Tim, arrived drunk and carrying two half full bottles of whiskey.

Tim came from a family where his father was an extremely hard working laborer. The rumor at school had it that his father once had a major run-in with the Passaic Police Department.

Tim didn't arrive drunk; he arrived "roaring drunk." He was loud, he was boisterous, and he offered a gulp of whiskey to anybody who wanted one.

In all candor, although all the boys had bragged at one time or another that they had drunk large quantities of liquor, probably 90% of them, including me, had never had a single drink. However, we were not going to be embarrassed at this party, not in front of the girls that were on the opposite side of the room, so we all drank a little of the whiskey and Tim drank more.

And then Tim got sick all over the rug and the drapes in the house. He then staggered to the front porch, laid down and fell sleep.

The boy in whose house the party was being held went into a state of panic. His mother's rug and draperies were probably ruined and she would kill him when she returned.

So here it was, the night of our great graduation, the night of our great joy, when all the boys were on their knees with scrub brushes washing the rug and the bottom of the drapes.

And what were most of the girls doing at that moment? Well, we realized they were no longer in the room. They were on the outside porch helping Tim; taking turns holding Tim's head in their lap and gently stroking him.

All of us then wondered if the secret to meeting girls and have them treat you nice is simply getting drunk, throwing up, and going to sleep on the porch. If it took those actions, I was never going to find a girl.

And that was how my junior high school years ended.

∗   ∗   ∗

Starting the very next day I began learning a more significant lesson from the copy of the Constitution that Mr. Cruise gave to me. Every day that summer, during dinner, my parents made me read aloud another part of the Constitution. We then discussed it, trying to understand its meaning. I often wonder how many of my classmates also had to read their copy of the Constitution. By the end of summer I realized that Passaic gave each of us a copy of the Constitution as an important symbol—it did not matter what country your parents or grandparents came from. The protection of the U.S. Constitution, coupled with continuing education was the key to a better future.

Passaic High School

In September 1947, my classmates and I entered the Passaic High School building for the first time—the famous "Hill Top High" of The Wonder Teams. The first day in high school we discovered that the building itself was a monstrosity. First of all, it was on one of the highest hills in Passaic. From the sidewalk to the building's front door we had to climb up stone steps that were very similar to the climb to the Lincoln Memorial in Washington, D.C.

Once we got in the building we realized that, unlike my junior high school, this building had no such thing as lockers where we could hang up our coats, store our boots in, and then lock them for safekeeping. Instead there were hooks on the hallway walls where we hung things and hoped that no one would take them. Also because the high school was located so far from the homes of some students, it was impractical for most of us to go home for lunch. Thus, they didn't allow anyone to leave the school during lunch. Instead, the "lunch hour" became the lunch "thirty minutes." To make matters worse there was no cafeteria in the school. Instead there were three "lunch wagons."

These lunch wagons were small wheeled carts that somehow miraculously appeared just before lunch hour (or should I say half hour). Standing behind each lunch counter was always the most sourpussed angry person, who would sell us a sandwich and give us grief as a dessert. Moreover, the only sandwiches that they ever sold were sliced egg (which always smelled putrid) or pressed ham. Could you imagine pressed ham—meat from a pig—being sold at a school located in a city which at that time had about a twenty-five percent Jewish population? And most of the Jews were "Orthodox," so they couldn't eat ham. The wagons also sold some milk and something they called cookies, which I'm sure were made in the automotive repair shop because they were made of absolute one hundred percent steel.

We were then assigned "home rooms." I was assigned Home Room 107 which was Mrs. Card's room who was head of the Spanish Department. The purpose of the home room was a place to go first thing in the morning to hear the announcements. But it also served another function. During the day everyone had two "study periods" when we didn't have an assigned class. During "study periods" we went back to our home room, sat in the back of the room while the teacher was teaching a class to the students in the front of the room. Obviously, it was not an easy place to study. Moreover, it was impossible to go to sleep during "study period" because the teacher would deliberately wake us up.

I had been spoiled in Number 11 School by having two separate gymnasiums, each of them a superb facility with very high ceilings and well equipped. In high school I discovered there was only one gym and it was tiny, the roof was about half the height of a normal gym's roof. The way we would have to play basketball is to shoot line drive shots; we couldn't arc the ball at all. Moreover, it was dingy and the locker rooms were atrocious. Obviously, no one would shower in them, and thus everyone, after being in gym class, walked around the rest of the day smelling from the sweat. To make matters worse, New Jersey law required every student to have one hour of gym every day of the school year.

Equaling the dinginess of the gym was the school auditorium. The seating was arranged in a full semi-circle around the stage. What this meant was that anybody that sat near the edge of the semi-circle couldn't see anything that was happening on the stage. Making matters worse, we were welcomed by the principal, Mr. Kennedy. After we got to know him, he was really a nice guy but he had one characteristic that was not easy to live with. He didn't talk, he mumbled. And he mumbled on the auditorium's stage; the stage, from which, even if you talked loud, nobody could hear you. So there we were sitting in this terribly designed auditorium watching this man who was obviously alive because you could see his lips moving, but no information was being transferred from him to the students.

The worst shock was the discovery that the high school also used an old building across the street as part of its classrooms. That building was called the "Annex," a small red building that only had a few rooms. It had been built before the Civil War, and therefore, it was almost one hundred years old and looked twice its age. Moreover, to get to the Annex within the few minutes we had between classes, we had to run like crazy down the long stairs, cross the street, and then enter the Annex. Even worse is when we had to run back to the main school for the next class, which meant running up that long flight of stairs and arriving out of breath, always late and then getting yelled at.

And because of the space limitations, only classes in tenth, eleventh, and twelfth grade were in the high school.

Yes, Passaic High's physical facility was terrible. However, I soon discovered that its teachers, its curriculum, and extracurricular activities were truly outstanding. I came to love it. In fact, as I moved on later in my life, I have been forever thankful for having had the privilege to learn in a school system where the Board of Education set such high standards.

*   *   *

Unlike Number 11 School, in high school we selected the classes we took provided we satisfied the city and state's minimum curriculum which included four years of English, history and of gym, plus two years of science and mathematics.

It quickly became obvious that I would be separated from many of my Number 11 school friends who had selected different courses. Moreover, there were two basic kinds of programs offered at Passaic High: "college preparatory" and "career oriented." About two thirds of the students took the career oriented courses which included, besides all the mandatory classes, options such as commercial typing, mechanical drawing, and many different vocational classes.

*   *   *

I quickly fell into a routine. I got to school early so I could shoot the breeze with my friends, the usual topic being "girls." Then classes would start, and the day would be hectic until about 2:30 when we got out of school. At that point I would rush to downtown Passaic which was about a mile walk, and go to the "Y" which opened at 3:00 p.m. and stayed open until 5:00 p.m. I would then go home for dinner, and rush back to the Y which again opened from 7:00 p.m. until 11:00 p.m.

The Y was a very important part of my growing up in Passaic. It had a great game room with three ping pong tables, two pool tables, four bowling alleys, as well as checkers, chess and other game room sports. Adjacent to the game room was the teenage lounge with a juke box, a dance floor and comfortable chairs. Upstairs was the Y's gym including a basketball court where anyone (even terrible players like me) could join teams. They also had a large auditorium where numerous plays and the Saturday night dances were held. In addition, the Y had many meeting rooms where the many high school fraternities and sororities held their meetings.

High school fraternities and sororities were very important social clubs. Almost all of my boy friends (with the exception of my friend Moishe) had joined one of the fraternities. You could always spot the people who were "pledged" because they wore specific color pins on their jackets or shirts indicating that they were pledging for a particular fraternity.

The purposes of the fraternities were—I never did find out what the purposes were. However, we had meetings, which almost always turned into screaming sessions, once a week at the Y. We also had sports competitions against the other fraternities, attempted to arrange joint meetings with sororities so we could learn how to dance (never had a successful one), and in general, we made life long friends.

In my hectic Y schedule, there was, of course, no time to do homework, but who was interested in doing homework anyway; we always had those two study periods to do our homework.

∗   ∗   ∗

In that first year in high school I took the geometry course which was taught by Mr. Ruland Anderson who was, without question, the finest teacher I ever had anywhere. Sitting directly in front of me was my cousin Marilyn.

One day while taking a particularly important geometry test, Marilyn secretly gave me a note asking for the answer to problem number seven. I truly loved my cousin and I would do anything for her so I scribbled the answer on a piece of paper, folded it two or three times and carefully handed it to her.

Unfortunately, the note slid out of Marilyn's hand and fell to the floor just as Mr. Anderson stood up at his desk and started circling through the isles as he always did during a test. He got to our aisle and saw the piece of paper on the floor and saw that it had my sloppy unintelligible handwriting on the outside of the note, that said "M" for Marilyn. He picked up the note and slowly turned to me.

(Before describing what happened next, it must be mentioned that Mr. Anderson was the strictest teacher I've ever known. He wouldn't give you one inch. If you made a mistake, you suffered for it.)

Mr. Anderson turned to me, with the still folded note in his hand. He said softly but loudly enough for both Marilyn and me to hear, "Robert, you must have lost this piece of paper. Put it back in your book." I reached over, took the still folded paper, put it in my book, not quite believing that he didn't realize that we were attempting to cheat.

He never again mentioned that note while I was in high school. However, I went back to Passaic High about eight years later to visit him and to describe how I was using the mathematics he taught me as an engineer at Douglas Aircraft Company. During that visit he said, "Bobby, I was pretty sure your note to your cousin involved cheating on the test. I hope you realized that if I had opened that note, both your cousin and you would have been expelled from the school."

Yes, Mr. Anderson was a great teacher, a very strict teacher, but he also knew when to "pull his punches."

*   *   *

There were only a few things I didn't like about PHS. One of them was the physics class taught by Mr. Clarke. Mr. Clarke was scheduled to retire the year that we were graduating. However, unfortunately, because he had been teaching physics for over thirty years using the same **textbook** that was written before 1920, it was an infuriating class. Since the book's publishing date, the atom had been split, atomic energy became a reality, and many of the basic precepts of modern physics changed the entire concept of physics that was in that obsolete textbook. And yet Mr. Clarke insisted that the textbook was totally accurate and that we must, in our answers to test questions, answer them based upon what we "learned" from it.

The disaster of learning from that obsolete physics book was, unfortunately, demonstrated to the entire world on one fateful day when a woman who we had never seen before walked into our physics class. She introduced herself and said that the Passaic Board of Education had decided to enter the National High School Physics Competition. Obviously, no one had told Mr. Clarke because he just sat down in an empty student's chair, with a shocked expression on his face.

The woman then said she was going to administer a physics test, and that the top three students from our school would then move on to a regional competition.

Well, the test was a fiasco. What we had learned in the textbook was so obsolete and so wrong that no one from our high school was invited to the regional competition—the only New Jersey high school that was not invited. It didn't phase Mr. Clarke one bit. He just continued to teach out of that textbook until the day he retired.

*　　　　　　*　　　　　　*

As all of us went through school we had to read a certain number of books. For example, in most grammar schools the students would read Robinson Crusoe. In high school, maybe Ivanhoe and maybe Shakespeare.

But I had managed to get to my senior year in high school without ever having read a single book in my entire life. I had faked every book assignment we ever had by either using classic comics as my source, or by questioning my classmates and learning the book's contents from them. Of course, none of my teachers realized that I had faked my way through including my Advanced English Class teacher, Mrs. Caskey—whose claim to fame was that her classroom was always the coldest classroom in the building; she called it "Caskey's Cooler." She did this by keeping the giant windows open all winter.

My lack of reading was not accidental. I simply didn't have the time since I was hanging out at the Y essentially seven days a week. (No, my parents never checked on my homework. And maybe they also stopped asking me to do many chores after I demonstrated my incompetence in emptying the tray from the ice box.)

Then a life changing event occurred while I had a bad case of the flu in the early spring of my senior year in high school. I was stuck home and had nothing to do. In my misery I scoured the house and found a book, "Fires of Spring" by author James Michener, and I sat down and I read it.

Fires of Spring was the story of a boy about my age, growing up in a carnival and learning about life, about girls and about sex—it was a coming of age book. And I fell in love with it.

I was amazed at how much I enjoyed reading it. In fact, I suddenly realized that, by having not read the assigned books in school, I had missed out on wonderful adventures. I couldn't wait until tomorrow when I would be well enough to go to school and talk to Mrs. Caskey about this.

The next morning I did feel well enough and I got to school early as usual and went to Caskey's Cooler. She was at her desk marking papers when I walked in. She looked up, and with a surprised look on her face, asked what I wanted.

I confessed that I had faked reading all the assigned books, not only from her class, but all the way back to first grade. I then explained that yesterday I had read my first book, the James Michener book, and it was an overwhelming eye opener. I then asked if she could give me a list of all the books I should have read up to now because now I wanted very much to read them.

As long as I live I will never forget her answer. She said, "That's not my job." She added, "And go to your home room now."

I was never more angry or upset at a teacher in my life. However, it didn't affect either my desire nor my intent.

For the past fifty years since I left high school I have read an average of more than two books a week every week. And if Mrs. Caskey is still among the living, I do wish her well and I am so pleased that she has retired from teaching.

*   *   *

Without question, my high school years were the years that I enjoyed the most. Everything sort of fit together so well, even when we had a crisis in the school system involving football.

After the war a new football coach arrived at the high school by the name of Manlio Boverini. During the first few years of his coaching, the football team did not perform very well. Each season had a losing record.

In Passaic football was very important. Passaic was a working class town surrounded by richer towns such as Clifton and East Rutherford. Thus, one of the few ways we were able to brag was by beating them in football games. Moreover, football success opened the door to many college scholarships for these athletes.

Little Known Fact—*"Passaic High School has had more graduates in the National Football League than any other high school in the country!"*

One day, near the end of our junior year in the early spring of 1949, the rumor started that the school system had decided to fire Coach Boverini. This rumor spread like wildfire throughout the school. Spontaneously in one classroom, almost all the students stood up and walked out into the hall chanting, "We want Bo, We want Bo." Then all the classrooms emptied and the classes were shut down. Students wandered throughout the halls chanting, "We want Bo."

The school's response was very interesting. They had apparently suspected something might happen and they immediately blocked all the doors that let people in and out of the school; blocked not by locks and not by large teachers. Instead, in front of each exit door was one of the school's smallest male teachers. And in front of the main front door of the school stood Mr. Ruland Anderson, a very skinny but very stern person.

The purpose of these "blocking teachers" was to prevent students from leaving the school. They were to stare down the students and calm the situation.

When my friends and I strutted up to Mr. Anderson and said, "We're leaving," he simply said, "Robert, turn around and take your friends back to class, NOW." Like little sheep, we turned around and went back to our classroom.

The commotion finally ended about two hours later and classes resumed. Whoever had made the decision to fire "Bo," if there was ever such a decision, had changed their mind. Mr. Boverini was reappointed as football coach for the next year, my senior year.

And to make this a Hollywood ending, in my senior year the Passaic football team was invincible. It went unbeaten. Moreover, some of my old friends from Number 11 School were stars on the team. For example, Frank Sorce played offense and defense (he was not very big, but was the best athlete I have ever known). Two other Number 11 School graduates were linemen on the team, Russ Carroccio and Irv Miller, and they led one of the most spectacular plays of the year.

I believe it was against Rutherford High, one of our arch enemies. Rutherford had won the coin toss and kicked off. I don't remember who caught it for Passaic, but in front of him was Russ Carroccio (I'm sure) and Irv Miller (I think it was). Carroccio was one of the biggest persons I had ever seen, well over six feet three, weighed over 250 pounds and strong as an ox, Miller was not as big but was a fierce competitor. The person with the ball ran along the right sideline directly behind stampeding Carroccio and Miller. The other team, seeing these "monsters" charging down the field like Erie Railroad locomotives, simply backed away and we ran for a touchdown.

Chants in the stadium during the last game of the year reflected the previous year's school uprising. The chant was, "We love Bo, we love Bo."

*   *   *

Football games during the previous year didn't have these "love chants." In fact, up to our annual game against East Rutherford, Passaic's football team hadn't scored any touchdowns.

To be very kind, the 1949 football team was inept. No, that really wasn't the problem. We really only had two problems in 1949. The first was that our team couldn't score any points. The second was that our opponent could score many points. In spite of these two small problems the entire student body still rallied around our team. Nevertheless, the Passaic Alumni Association was unhappy. At the beginning of the year, they had bought a new cannon that was to be fired each time Passaic would score a touchdown. Prior to the first game of the year, the cannon was filled with confetti that would be spattered all over when it was fired. But we didn't score a touchdown.

Each week the alumni carried this fully loaded heavy cannon to the game. Each week they waited in order to pull the lanyard to fire it. Each week they carried the cannon back out of the game unfired because we couldn't score any points.

During the late season game with East Rutherford a minor miracle did happen. The Passaic offense began to gain yards. In the press box, one of my more popular classmates, Richie Werksman, had been hired to write articles about the football games for the three local newspapers (The Passaic Herald News, The Paterson Call, and Passaic Eagle). For the first time in many games, Richie felt excitement as our team moved the ball down the field.

Then it finally happened. Our team scored!

Richie worked feverishly typing the statistics of this wonderful first Passaic touchdown of the year. He recorded the yards. He recorded who made the runs. He wrote wonderful praise about the great moment when Passaic crossed the goal line. As he typed the last sentence, he looked back at the typewriter, rather proud of his accomplishment. He then looked up at the field and in passing, noticed that the standby ambulance was leaving the football field. He ignored it because it didn't affect his story which he was sending to the three newspapers.

The next day he went down to visit the only newspaper that published on Sunday, the Passaic Eagle, and walked into the editor's office. As soon as he walked in he realized that the editor was furious at him. The editor screamed at him, "Where were you? What game were you watching? Why did I have to read about a major news story concerning Passaic in a New York newspaper?" Richie didn't know what the editor was talking about.

What he didn't know was that at that great moment when the touchdown was scored the alumni finally fired the cannon in celebration. The cannon, which had been loaded with confetti many weeks before, made an incredible boom that echoed all over the stadium. Everyone heard it, except Richie, who was totally engrossed in writing the touchdown story. This ace reporter also didn't hear the frightened scream, nor saw the blood.

What the ace reporter missed was that the cannon didn't quite work properly. Instead of the "shot" coming out of the cannon as loose confetti and being spread all over the field, it had solidified over the long wait for the first touchdown. It shot out of the cannon as a solid mass, and it hit and wounded Jackie Thompson, one of the more popular cheerleaders, slightly above the knee. As Richie was typing how many yards were gained and who made the score, people began giving Jackie first aid and the ambulance charged onto the field. Richie never saw this. The emergency team stopped the bleeding with pressure and drove her away. The only thing Richie slightly noticed were the tail lights of the ambulance leaving.

*   *   *

The loss of the newspaper scoop probably affected Richie's future career. After graduation from high school he went off to college and instead of becoming a journalist, he became an outstanding lawyer. He is now a senior official in the U.S. State Department.

And the one thing I'm sure of, he now always keeps one eye open to what's happening around him as he performs his important government functions.

Passaic Stadium

Passaic played in a stadium surrounded by ten foot high concrete walls that had barbed wire along the top. However, over the years the barbed wire has been broken in many places. The stadium was located adjacent to the Erie Railroad tracks, just between Passaic and Passaic Park.

Before every game, large crowds of us high school boys would stand on the other side of the railroad tracks away from the stadium. Between us and the stadium wall there were always several of the high school teachers. We waited and they waited.

When the teams finally came on the field just prior to kick-off, for some reason I'll never understand, all the teachers walked away from the wall. At that instant, there was the mad dash by all the boys to the wall. The stronger guys managed to get to the top of the wall. They helped the weaker guys climb to the wall and hundreds of students climbed over the wall to save the $0.35 admission fee.

The few times I was inside the stadium early (sometimes I sold the Football Programs for the games), I had the thrill of watching the youthful hoard charging over the walls. It was truly an amazing sight.

Of course, the high school girls didn't participate. They had already paid their entrance fee. But they cheered on the boys from the Passaic side of the grandstands (from the wooden bleachers; the very cold stone bleachers we left for our opponents).

I don't think anyone who charged over the wall ever did it in order to save the few pennies admission. We did it solely because it was our little act of defiance against the administration of the school system that 1950 had again not approved the plans for a new high school which the city so desperately needed.

*   *   *

Passaic finally did build a new high school. It was on a large site where in 1873 Charles Paulison had built a real castle with turrets and towers. Unfortunately, he went broke that year because of the National Depression and the castle remained uncompleted. Thirty years later the city of Passaic bought the entire property, and after installing a roof on the castle, it became the foreboding Passaic City Hall.

On one corner of the castle property was where, in 1939, the Julius Forstmann Library had been built (corner of Passaic Avenue and Gregory Avenue). Finally, many years after I graduated from high school, the castle was demolished and the new Comprehensive Passaic High School, and a new City Hall, were built on the property.

Yes, there has been considerable progress in the city of Passaic!

CHAPTER 8

Friends and Special Acquaintances

One great thing about being brought up in Passaic, is that most people developed very close friendships with lots of their classmates.

I was so blessed. In fact, even today, fifty years after high school, I receive about ten phone calls every week from different friends of my high school days.

However, such close friends were usually limited to your own ethnic group or your own neighborhood. In addition to these tight circles of friends, you also developed "special acquaintances," from other ethnic groups or neighborhoods.

For example, Russ Carroccio, the football and track star, was certainly from a different ethnic group than I. We never did play or socialize together. However, he was one of my special acquaintances. How did it come to be? Very simple. I betrayed one of my friends in favor of Russ. On our track team, Russ was the star shotputter. He always led the team in this strenuous competition.

It was the end of the track season and at the annual team meeting the vote was about to be taken on who had been the most valuable track athlete that year. Certainly, the odds on favorite was Louis Kleinman, who was the most successful athlete on the team. He ran the grueling 440 yard "dash" and won almost every one of his races. Moreover, he was very helpful to the other track team members, urging them on and helping them train. Everyone thought that Louis would be proclaimed by acclamation to be the outstanding track star of the year.

When the coach asked if there were any nominations besides Louis, there was total silence in the room. As the coach waited a polite few seconds for the expected unanimous vote for Louis, I raised my hand and said, "I nominate Russ Carroccio."

The entire room seemed stunned. It wasn't that Russ was unpopular, but that Louis was extremely popular. One of my closer friends, for example, Maish Gendes who I hung out with in high school all the time, and was the second shotputter on the team, couldn't believe that I wasn't going to vote for our mutual close friend, Louis.

The coach looked at me like I was crazy. However, for some reason, maybe because I was such a lousy runner, he always had looked at me as if I was crazy. He asked if anyone would second the nomination.

You must remember that Russ was a very big guy and no one wanted to be on the wrong side of him. Moreover, many of the people on the track team were from the Second Ward where Russ lived and were also Italian, same as Russ. Thus, one of Russ's friends, who would have never thought to nominate Russ, seconded the nomination.

The coach again looked stunned. It was put to a secret ballot and Louis Klineman was elected by a vote of 24 to 1 as the year's Most Valuable Track Athlete.

No, I'm not going to admit whether Russ's lone vote came from me, from his friend who seconded the nomination or from Russ himself. However, it's interesting that only one of us voted for him.

After the election, Maish asked me why in the world I had nominated Russ. I answered that there were two separate reasons. First, Russ worked hard to become a better shotputter even though perhaps he didn't help the rest of his teammates as much as Louis. And second, in order to get to my house on Oak Street, I had to walk past Russ's very tough neighborhood.

Maish didn't understand the second reason at all. Obviously, he wouldn't understand it, he was well over six feet and very muscular whereas I was a small kid and didn't weigh 110 pounds. So each time I had to walk up Monroe Street, past Russ's Italian neighborhood to get to my house from the Y, I did have some fear in my heart.

And it worked. After the track meeting the word went out from Russ that I was a friend of his and from that day forward I was never hassled nor bothered as I walked up Monroe Street. Thus, the nomination of Russ Carroccio was proper and I'm proud that I did it (and yes, I now will admit it, I cast the one vote for Russ).

After graduating from Passaic High, Russ Carroccio was a star tackle at the University of Virginia's football team. He went on to play in the NFL for the New York Giants and Philadelphia Eagles. When the famed coach of the Green Bay Packers, Vince Lombardi, saw Russ play he named him "The Sicilian Bomb Thrower" because of his exceptional speed for such a huge man.

*   *   *

The post war economic boom had certainly helped my father's and uncle's store. In fact, they decided to move the store to downtown Passaic. My father explained to me that whenever you move a retail business you lose a lot of the neighborhood customers, and you could only hope that in the busier downtown area you would gain enough new customers to make up for it.

As part of this increasing prosperity we decided we could finally move out of the tenement where I had lived my entire life. We were going to move to Passaic Park—to the part of town where the rich kids lived.

Unfortunately, I wasn't going to live like the rich kids. In fact, my parents had rented another flat. It was located on top of a candy store on the corner of Ascension Street and Main Avenue. This was an old railroad type of flat that had rooms one after another with a narrow "aisle" as the hall so you could walk between the rooms. However, to me it was true luxury. I was finally, after fifteen years, getting my own room.

However, moving posed a new problem. I almost always went to the Y after school and on Saturdays and Sundays. However, it was too far to walk from Passaic Park to the Y. Thus, I began to take public transportation (there was no public transportation where I lived on Oak Street). In the process I discovered one of the strange laws of economics. There were two identical buses that went down Main Street. One was Number 74 which charged seven cents to get to downtown Passaic. The other bus was Number 112 and they charged ten cents for traveling the identical route to downtown Passaic. The buses were the same. The company that owned the buses (Public Service) was the same, and yet there were two different fares.

After investigating I found out that the more expensive bus ran from Newark to Paterson. They wanted to discourage local riders (like me going from Passaic Park to Passaic) to save the seats for the intercity riders, so they charged us a higher fare.

Many times in my career I have used this basic lesson in economics learned from riding the Passaic buses. Whenever I had to set prices for company products, I would think of Bus 74 and 112. In fact, my company once offered two similar products but one was aimed at a niche market and the other at a more general market. I named the first product Model 74 (for which we charged less) and the other product Model 112.

*   *   *

In high school I was blessed with a very large group of friends. Many of them were intellectuals—I defined "intellectuals" as those that actually did homework at home. Others were like me—hanging out at the Y and having a hell of a lot of fun. But all my friends and acquaintances had one thing in common: We'd end up at the end of most days at Rutt's Hut.

It is really hard to explain what Rutt's Hut is. In fact, in 1999, public television had a special program on "Famous Hotdog Stands in America." And one of them shown—the only one shown on the east coast besides Nathan's at Coney Island—was Rutt's Hut just outside of Passaic, New Jersey.

Yes, Rutt's Hut was a hotdog stand, but it was really much more. Its hotdogs were made in boiling oil. (We didn't know and could care less about cholesterol in the 1940's. Even today, when everyone knows about cholesterol, they still make their hotdogs boiled in oil.)

The Rutt's Hut building was composed of two parts. The front was a counter where you stood up and ate your food (normally, four or five deep would be eating). In the rear part of the building you could sit down and be offered the same food.

In the 1940's, long before there was McDonalds, there was Rutt's Hut which was in fact, a fast food restaurant. No matter what you ordered, it was half cooked, overcooked or undercooked, but delivered to you within a few seconds. To accomplish this the countermen used their own language which their customers also quickly learned. For example, a "ripper" was a hotdog where they used a fork to rip open its side and then boil it in oil. The advantage of ordering a ripper is that the inside would be thoroughly cooked. The disadvantage was that when you bit into this delicious part of Americana, you would immediately burn the roof of your mouth. They also used other strange words like "PC" which meant coffee in a paper cup, and "Yahoo" which meant a chocolate soda.

Rutt's Hut was the place where you went with or after a date. It was noisy and crowded. On the 1999 PBS program, they interviewed a couple who had started going to Rutt's Hut in my generation in the 1940's. That couple pointed out that the enormous parking lot at Rutt's Hut was where everybody went to "make out." Well, I'm almost ashamed to admit it, but I never knew that, nor did I ever "make out" at Rutt's Hut.

∗   ∗   ∗

Rutt's Hut was the meeting place for my large group of friends and acquaintances, each of whom were different in small but important ways. However, there was one of my friends that was a member of my high school fraternity and was a truly unique individual. This was my friend, Lenny, who everybody called "The Duck."

Quack-Quack

Pandemonium prevails.

The chairman of the AZA high school fraternity keeps appealing for order, attempting to have the membership calm down and carefully consider this important matter.

The year is 1949. World War II has been over for four years. Prosperity is returning and high school fraternities are alive and well. At least they were up to the start of this meeting.

The meeting's chairman feels somewhat relaxed even though the shouting continues. He has convinced the membership not to castrate Lenny. Moreover, he had stopped the membership from voting to hang him, to tar and feather him, and even convinced them not to drag Lenny through the streets. However, the chairman, who was perhaps Lenny's only remaining friend, didn't think he could control the mob from taking its due revenge upon that miserable bastard.

And in the middle of this turmoil, what is Lenny saying? In a calm voice, he keeps repeating: "So I forgot. What's the big deal? So I forgot."

A bit of background: For thirteen years our fraternity had organized one of the high school's premier social event—the Turkey Hop—always held on Thanksgiving Night at the Ritz Ballroom in beautiful Downtown Passaic. This was the major cultural event of the year for my high school crowd. Every year it was a complete sellout, every year it was eagerly looked forward to, every year it was held on Thanksgiving Night.

Except this year.

This year we had assigned Lenny to hire the Ritz Ballroom, and our membership had just discovered that the owner of the Ritz Ballroom had waited for Lenny to sign the contract for the Turkey Hop. And waited. And waited. Finally he gave up, and rented the Ballroom to another group for a bingo game on Thanksgiving Night.

Now Lenny just sits there, calmly repeating: "So I forgot, big deal." The membership howls for the blood of this heartless creature.

Cooler heads finally prevail. The membership finally voted on the following resolution: "LET IT BE KNOWN TO ALL MEN OF THE WORLD, LENNY IS, FROM THIS TIME FORWARD, EXPELLED FROM THE HUMAN RACE." The resolution is carried 28 to 0. Even Lenny voted for it!

Well that was many years ago when Lenny was like the character in the Lil' Abner comic strip—he always had a black cloud over his head. We had nick-named him "The Duck" because, although he was always followed by the black cloud, he somehow managed to "swim" away without getting his feathers wet.

But now it is 1970, twenty years after graduating from Passaic High, and the "Duck" has grown up and become a mature, successful business man.

We are at a reunion, in Washington, D.C., of former Passaic friends. Many of Lenny's old friends are present; none of us had seen him during the last twenty years. Lenny arrives a little late, but all of us notice that he has obviously undergone an incredible metamorphosis.

He is smartly dressed in a three piece suit, obviously well educated, and certainly a man of the world. We are all impressed—the little black cloud apparently no longer follows him around.

His new maturity becomes even more evident after we sat down at this lovely seafood restaurant. All of us are indeed impressed when Lenny reaches for the wine list, and in a carefully cultured French, reads off the names of the wines.

Unfortunately, as he reads the wine names, he holds the wine list over the lit candle on the table—the wine list promptly catches fire.

Lenny calmly extinguishes the blaze by dipping the burning wine list into the crab soup—not his soup, but mine.

Everyone is saying, "Lenny, didn't you see the candle?" Lenny's response is "What's the big deal? So I forgot."

Once a duck, always a duck.

EPILOGUE—In honor of Lenny's 50th birthday in 1983, I contacted eight members of our former high school fraternity and requested that we vote on rescinding the old resolution and allow Lenny to again become a member of the human race.

We took a secret ballot. The motion was defeated 9 to 0. (Yes, even I voted against it.) Lenny remains forever expelled from the human race—he remains The Duck.

POST EPILOGUE—The book editor has just informed me that Lenny, who now lives in Boston, was recently ill. The editor said it was somehow related to Lenny's heart. He then asked if I would want to revise my description of Lenny as "heartless." I told the editor I am shocked at the lack of knowledge of the greater Boston medical profession. Any doctor from Passaic, particularly if the doctor was a former member of my high school fraternity, knows that Lenny does not have a heart—in Lenny's chest instead of a heart, there is an overcooked, still pulsating RUTT'S HUT HOTDOG!

A "RIPPER."

CHAPTER 9

Girls, Girls, Girls!

During my high school years I finally realized that the Passaic girls were subdivided into two different groups. The "Goddesses" were the girls who in no way would I ever possibly approach and talk to. They were obviously much superior to me.

The other group of girls were "Queens." Although they weren't quite at the level of the Goddesses, they also were in a group who would never go out on a date with me. Occasionally they may have talked to me but they were truly untouchable.

There was one exception. She was a wonderfully wholesome girl by the name of "PH" who became not only a friend to me, but a friend to all the other guys who hung out at the Y.

PH was the first girl that I ever had a date with. For five days I walked to the pay phone in the Y and for five days I walked away from it, not having worked up the nerve to call her. Finally I did telephone her and asked her to go to the 1947 Turkey Hop with me. And to my shock and total surprise she said "yes."

For this great occasion—not only was it a date for the major dance on Thanksgiving Night, but also since it was my first date—my father let me pick out a new pair of shoes from his store. I then realized that I didn't really know PH very well and I wasn't sure whether she was taller than me, but I thought she was, so I picked out a pair of shoes with one inch high red rubber soles that had cleats in them. I also bought a new sport jacket, a maroon cardigan jacket that I wore for the next four years.

The great day finally arrived and after having a great Thanksgiving lunch and going to the Passaic High football game (which they lost), I rushed home, took a shower, took another shower, and then to make absolutely certain, I took a third shower. I finally got dressed and began to walk from Second Ward to downtown Passaic. PH lived on the lower side of Passaic about four blocks below the railroad tracks. When I finally got to her house I was a little winded and was worried that maybe I should have taken a fourth shower.

I finally walked up the steps to her house, knocked on the door and her mother came to the door. I was petrified, but PH rescued me and off we went to the dance at the Ritz Ballroom.

Then I realized I had made two major disasters. I had never told PH that I didn't know how to dance. However, she being one of the sweetest people in the world, said she would teach me how to dance. It was then I discovered the second disaster; the red rubber cleated shoes made it impossible to move your feet on the dance floor. So there I was, clumsy as hell, not being able to dance, and totally embarrassed.

But I really did have a wonderful time anyway and thanked PH profusely when I dropped her off at her house.

That was the one and only date that I ever had with a girl from Passaic.

*   *   *

PH used to come to the Y several days a week and became a "sister" to me and all my friends. Whenever we had problems about girls, we would approach PH, who would give us advice. Unfortunately, because we all treated her as a sister, I'm afraid she didn't have as many dates as she really deserved. She was a sweet wonderful girl and was handicapped because everybody knew she was a sweet wonderful girl.

After high school, PH married one of my close high school friends and now it is well over forty years later and they appear to be happy and are still living in Passaic.

PH, if you read this book, I want you to know that I'll always love you in that special way that anyone would love a very close sister.

*   *   *

Very few of my friends dated any Passaic girls because we realized it was impossible to date Goddesses and Queens. We were mostly slobs and we knew it. However, surrounding Passaic were many other cities and most of us found girls to date from those other cities. In this "hunt" for girls we found two girls who were very important throughout our high school and college years.

Each of the girls had a unique talent that was mandatory whenever we had parties at one of our friends' houses. One of the girls, from Clifton, by the name of "R" played the piano beautifully, so it was important for one of our friends to date her so that we would have a live music at our parties. Her masterpiece was "Clare De Lune" which became sort of the theme song of our parties.

Over time she dated several different friends including Gideon, Alan, Freddie, and others. She was a wonderful young lady and always mixed well with the other girls who we invited to the parties.

There was another girl from a different part of Clifton who also was mandatory to have a date with one of my friends whenever we had a party. The reason it was mandatory was because of her father's business. Before describing this let me first provide some background.

Most of my friends were Jewish whose immigrant parents or grandparents had first lived on the east side of New York City. On the sidewalks on the east side of New York were many pushcarts selling various foods from the old country. One of the more popular delicacies, which my friends and I learned to love, was eating pickles directly from the pickle barrel. During my youth when we visited the east side we could buy a good pickle—which we called a "half sour pickle"—for two cents.

So now you know why it was important to date "E." Her father owned the largest pickle making company in New Jersey and provided she had a date for our party we would have an unlimited number of pickles.

Fortunately, E was not only a great pickle provider but a wonderful girl who you were able to talk to and we enjoyed her company. She certainly was not like the Goddesses and Queens of Passaic.

Of course, all the other girls at our party always thought it was quite a coincidence that both R and E always attended our parties. We never divulged the reason for that coincidence.

*   *   *

In 1990 my high school graduating class had its 40th reunion. Unfortunately, the number of people attending our reunion was unexpectedly high, and therefore, the room was very overcrowded and hot.

About half way through the evening I decided to get up and walk out into the hall so that I could get some fresh air. There standing in the hall were four of the Queens along with three of the Goddesses in our high school class. They were chatting among themselves and then one of them said, "Hi Bob."

Well, there I was, fifty-seven years old, forty years after graduating from PHS, president of a major corporation, married for thirty-seven years with four grown children. And yet I was dumbstruck that these heaven sent girls from Passaic High were actually talking to me. I was truly nervous.

I walked over to them and we made small talk. Not only did the girl who said "Hi Bob" talk to me, but all of the Queens and Goddesses talked to me. I really couldn't believe it!

I confessed to them how during my high school years I really wanted to go out on a date with any one of them who might have accepted me, but I knew it was an impossible desire.

They all looked at me and almost in unison said, "Why didn't you call me, Bob? I would have loved to have gone out with you. I sat home many Saturday nights because no one would call me."

It was an overwhelming shock to me that the Queens and Goddesses of my high school were wonderful people to talk to and had the normal desires for dates and friends like all us commoners.

*   *   *

A few of my friends actually did date girls from Passaic. However, strange rules were slowly generated regarding such dates. Passaic girls who dated one of my friends, even if they only went out once, became that guy's "property." From that time on, no other friend was allowed to ever ask that girl for a date.

For example, during high school I really had a major "crush" on a girl named "T." She was a brilliant student, small in stature and unusual in my generation, she wore glasses. And I really liked her.

Unfortunately, in our sophomore year my friend, Alan, had dated her, so she became "Alan's property." Therefore, all during high school, although I recognized that she wasn't a Goddess or Queen—after all she had dated one of my fellow degenerates—I couldn't possibly ask her out on a date.

A few years after graduating from high school, during summer break from college, I received a phone call from T. It was a most welcome and wonderfully warm phone call. In fact, as I remember it, it was the first phone call I had ever received from a girl (that just wasn't done during the 1940's and 1950's). Near the end of this warm phone conversation, she asked if I'd like to meet her at the Y that night. After hemming and hawing, I made a lame excuse that I couldn't do it but we'd get together "someday."

I never did call her back, but I always wondered if I had and asked her on a real date, would she have accepted. After all, she was Alan's property.

My Polite Friend

Yes, I had friends that were big and strong and others who were per-haps a little crazy. I had friends who actually did their homework and others who were bums like me. But among all my friends, I only had one that was really brought up to be polite and to always respect his eld-ers. His name was Josh (no that wasn't really his name, however, as will be obvious from the following story, it would be very "difficult" to use his real name).

It's probably true that in every group of teenagers there is one who always wore clean clothes, had good manners, didn't curse, kept his shoes shined, and never got into trouble. That, of course, was Josh. But Josh, had the same teenage hormones surging in his arteries as the rest of my friends.

It was a typical Saturday night during our junior year in high school. We all had dates with out-of-town girls, and there were four couples squeezed into my '38 Chevy. It really wasn't much of a date. All we did was go to the Passaic Y and shoot some pool, play some ping pong and watch the girls dance together in the teenage lounge. However, we drove all the girls back to their homes in my car.

Because we were always scrounging for money, we tended to choose the shortest route to drop everybody off. We first dropped off my date. Then we drove to the house of Lenny's and Moish's dates and they walked them to their doors. Thus, left in the car were all four of us with only Josh's date to still be dropped off.

Before proceeding, it should be mentioned that although he was a near perfect teenager, he did have one imperfection. When Josh got extremely excited he tended to stutter. However, this rarely occurred because Josh had one of those wonderful calm temperaments.

We got to Josh's date's house on Clifton Avenue. It was one of the few neighborhoods in Clifton that looked a lot like Passaic. The houses were close together, and in fact the houses were constructed from the design sold in the Sears Roebuck Catalog. Many of the houses in Passaic and Clifton were part of prefabricated housing you could buy through the Sears Catalog and have them built on your lot.

These types of houses tended to be built on smaller than usual lots that had a small driveway but without a garage. Thus, parking in front of them became difficult because there was very little curb space. But I did find a parking space about two houses past where Josh's date lived.

Josh walked his date to the front door and discovered the house was dark and locked. The girl, of course, had her own key and Josh and the girl went into the house.

For five minutes, for ten minutes, for fifteen minutes we waited.

Just then we saw headlights of another car approaching. It was the girl's parents driving home and they pulled into the driveway. It is worth noting that Clifton Avenue is a very heavily traveled road, and thus it's difficult to hear in the house that the parents' car had just arrived.

These Sears Roebuck houses were typically laid out that the living room faced the front door. Moreover, since the proudest possession in most working people's homes was their living room sofa, the room was laid out so that the sofa was directly visible when someone walked in the front door.

And as her parents opened the front door, sitting on the couch was Josh and their daughter, and she no longer had any clothes on above the waist.

When Josh saw the parents he leaped up and said, "P P P P P P P PARDON ME." And he ran towards the back door. He opened the back door and in full stride ran right through the back porch screen door which had been locked, around the two neighbors' houses and leaped into the back seat of our car. Part of the wire mesh of the screen door was still stuck on Josh's face when he came into the car.

As we all turned and stared at him looking at his bloodied face, he said, "P P P P P P P Parents!"

We then started the car and drove off while Josh, still stuttering, attempted to tell us all the gory details.

No we didn't ever find out how the girl and her parents resolved the matter. Moreover, Josh never again dated that girl. But from that day forward whenever any of us saw Josh, we always greeted him by saying, "P P P P P Parents!" And Josh would always respond with a sweet remembering smile on his face.

The Senior Prom

As in most high schools, our Senior Prom was the most important social event of the year. A special committee was formed to transform the dirty, dingy high school gym into an elegant dance floor. They did this by hanging streamers and other decorations. Of course, I never told them that the only thing they succeeded in doing was making the dingy, ugly, old gym look like a dingy, dirty, old gym with streamers and decorations.

I was going to go to the special event with my current girl friend, Vivian, who lived in Morristown. When the magic day arrived, I first drove up Main Avenue into Clifton where the large cemetery was. On the cemetery grounds there was a greenhouse called "McKay's" that sold orchids. Almost everybody bought their orchids from McKay's. I cleaned up my old '38 Chevy, picked up my date, and off we went to Passaic High School. Almost all my friends were there including Gideon, Alan, Maish, Moishe, Charlie, and so many others. It was a glorious evening.

Following the prom we went on the traditional drive to the Atlantic Ocean to watch the sunrise come up and then we drove our dates home and dropped them off.

My friends and I had developed a new custom following dates. We would end up at the Rainbow Diner, which was on Main Avenue in Passaic Park. The diner was a place where only the guys could attend.

We could almost never bring our dates there except if we received very special permission from the other guys. At the Rainbow Diner, on most Saturday nights after we had dropped off our dates, we'd get together and tell the world's greatest lies on how we "made out" on our dates. Everybody knew everybody else was lying but the purpose of it was to try to think of something that could really shock your friends.

You gotta remember this was a different generation. Even though we were in high school and even seniors in high school, none of the guys had very much knowledge about sex. And thus, our lies were full of inaccuracies about things we really didn't know, but really wanted to know.

*   *   *

It is now more than fifty years later. I spend all my free time at a marina on the Chesapeake Bay. The boat owners include executives of the World Bank, high military officers, successful businessmen, etc. But it really is very much like Passaic in 1950.

Invariably, the women and men tend to sit and gab on different parts of the dock. And the men's conversation always ends up being about girls they've known. And I hear the same stories—the same lies—about sex that I originally heard at the Rainbow Diner fifty years before. Some things never change.

CHAPTER 10

Potpourri

The Boy Scouts

In the 1940's the Boy Scouts was a different organization than it is today. Perhaps the biggest difference was that you couldn't join the scouts until you were twelve years old and most of us stayed in scouting until we were fifteen or sixteen, i.e. into our high school years.

In Passaic there were many different scout troops. Most of the troops only contained one ethnic group of boys because that troop normally met in churches, which meant that the local boys in that church area joined that troop.

There was one notable exception. For some mysterious reason the Salvation Army sponsored a boy scout troop that was almost entirely Jewish. This was Troop 29 which met each week at the Salvation Army building.

The staff of the Salvation Army were wonderful hosts. They let our troop use their recreational facilities at any time we wanted. They had a full gymnasium as well as excellent bowling alleys. In fact, most of us developed very fond relationships with the officers of the Salvation Army. This close relationship of a Jewish boy scout troop with the Salvation Army sometimes had unusual consequences.

For example, during the Christmas season in downtown Passaic, there were many Salvation Army kettles with people ringing bells to raise funds. These kettles were located outside most of the major stores all along Main Avenue and Lexington Avenue. Of course, there were more kettles than there were Salvation Army personnel. Thus, they were most grateful when our boy scout troop volunteered to staff some of them.

So there I was on a freezing December afternoon standing in front of the giant Woolworth store (corner of Jefferson Street and Lexington Avenue), ringing the bell with all my might. I was determined that I was going to raise the most money of anyone from our troop (which included outdoing my friend Moishe for this honor). In my enthusiasm, ringing the bell, I suddenly realized that my very religious Jewish grandfather was standing directly in front of me.

My grandfather just kept looking at me and never saying anything. He was on his way to his "Shul" on Hope Avenue for evening prayers. And here was his oldest grandson, who had been Bar Mitzvahed just one year before, standing next to a Salvation Army kettle and ringing its bell. He stood there and looked and looked.

He finally turned away and walked down toward Hope Avenue. I was certainly unnerved by this and didn't quite know what I should do. Should I go to my grandfather's apartment and wait for him to come home from Shul and explain why I was doing it? Should I say nothing? Should I tell my father? All these thoughts were running through my head as I rang the bell over and over and people kept putting money into the kettle.

I decided to say nothing and not bring up the subject with my grandfather. However, I saw my grandfather several times a week and I was sure he would bring it up.

It just so happened that Sunday my parents had driven my grandparents to our house for dinner. All through dinner I was expecting my grandfather to raise the question of the Salvation Army and why his grandson was ringing the bell for their kettle. But he never mentioned it.

And in fact, he never mentioned it. And I never brought it up with him. Thus, I had no idea what was going through his mind as he stood there for that long time watching me.

And then it happened again.

Now it was a gorgeous spring day and the Major in the Salvation Army asked me if I could help their band. I told him I would like to but that I had absolutely no musical training and didn't know how to play any instrument.

What the Major needed was somebody to play the bass drum as the Salvation Army's four piece band would march up and down Main Street until they would finally stop and give a little speech hoping to convince some people to come to their mission. The Major insisted that he could teach me how to play the bass drum, "If you can count to three, you can be a bass drum player."

So there I was wearing a Salvation Army jacket walking behind the other three members of the band plus the "preacher" who led the whole "parade" to the beat of my base drum, 1, 2, 3 BOOM, 1, 2, 3 BOOM, 1, 2, 3 BOOM…We marched to my beat as we walked the entire Lexington Avenue and came back. We finally stopped in front of the busiest shopping corner in the city, the corner where Ben Krone's Men's Store was on Lexington Avenue and Madison Avenue, directly across from the Erie Railroad Station. When we stopped I realized that following me was a little old man—MY GRANDFATHER. How long he had been behind me I don't know, but when I saw him he was standing there just staring at me just like he stared at me at Christmas time by the kettle.

When we stopped marching and stood in front of the Ben Krone Store, the trumpet player and the trombone player started a rousing rendition of the Salvation Army's theme song called "Bringing in the Sheaves." The song also had a solo part for me, the base drummer. Those of us that didn't play wind instruments were expected to loudly sing the song. Thus, the preacher and the person playing the chimes, and I began to sing as loudly as we could, "Bringing in the Sheaves…BOOM (my

base drum)...Bringing in the Sheaves...BOOM...We shall come rejoic-
ing...BOOM...Bringing in the Sheaves...BOOM...BOOM...BOOM."

My grandfather watched this event with unblinking eyes. When we
started to sing he took a step back and when I gave my three mighty hits
on the bass drum, he stepped back still further until he then turned and
walked off.

And again he didn't mention it when I saw him later.

Finally, about six months later I couldn't suppress knowing what my
grandfather thought about these activities. I asked him, "Grandpa, do
you remember me ringing the bell and playing the bass drum?" He spun
and looked right at me and he shook his head yes. I asked, "What did
you think?"

He stared at me with his black eyes and said, "I knew they weren't
paying you because you didn't have any drumming skill and didn't have
any voice to sing. I also knew that you hadn't joined the Salvation Army
because you were still going to Hebrew School. So after watching you
and thinking about it, I concluded that the only explanation was that
you believed that these people did good work and you were volunteering to help them to raise money so that they could do more good work.
Therefore, I turned around and walked away. Bobby, I was really proud
of you."

I stood there in amazement. He had so correctly understood my help
to the Salvation Army.

America First

In 1949, the year before I graduated from high school, my grandfather finally graduated from high school. He had started night school in
the year he came to America in 1900 and he had been going to school
for forty-nine straight years, first graduating grammar school and now
finally high school.

In celebration of this great accomplishment my father arranged a small party in the Ritz Restaurant which was next door to the Montauk Theater in downtown Passaic. The party included several friends of my grandfather as well as some family members.

Whenever there is a joyous Jewish celebration there is always "schnapps"—whiskey—and my grandfather carefully put his three fingers on the side of a glass—a wide glass—and poured the schnapps to the height of the width of his three fingers. We then took turns toasting him and he sipped a little bit of his "three fingers."

Finally it was time for my grandfather to make a speech. He asked me to stand up and proudly told everybody that I was going to be the first of his family ever to go to college (obviously, he didn't know I had no such plans). And then he treated me like a man—he shook my hand for the first time. In front of everybody he said, "Bobby, you're going to be the first to go to college. Do you think you're the smartest in this family?" I looked at him, somewhat embarrassed, and said, "No Grandpa, I don't think I'm the smartest."

He looked me in the eye and said, "Who do you think is the smartest in this family?" My response was, "Grandpa I don't know, who is it?"

He stared me in the eye but with a big smile on his face, he said, "Well, let me tell you who is the smartest. I am."

I just couldn't resist. I said, "Grandpa, why do you think you're the smartest in this family?"

His answer was a classic, which I will never forget. He said, "I'm the smartest because I chose America!"

All the friends and relatives stood up and applauded him and he had the biggest broadest smile on his face and he was certainly correct. If he hadn't chose to escape from Russia and come to America, we would have all perished in the Holocaust. Yes indeed. He was the smartest in the family.

When all the applause finally stopped, he turned to me and he said, "Bobby, I want you to make me one promise that you'll always keep." I said, "Grandpa, whatever you want me to promise I will certainly always keep that promise."

He said, "Bobby, I never want you to forget that America saved us and we all owe an enormous debt of gratitude to America." He then told the story that during the 1930's when he lost his business and all his money in the great depression, the IRS tax people hounded him. And that even today, 1949, he was still paying off the back taxes they claimed that he owed, even though he was sure he didn't owe any.

He said, "Even with this bad experience with the U.S. government it's still the greatest country on earth. It's the only country where you could go to sleep and be sure someone isn't going to break down your door in the middle of the night and drag you away." He said, "Bobby, the promise I want you to make is that whenever you have choices to make you will always choose America first. Never make a choice for money, for love, for prestige that will in any way violate your promise to me that you will always choose America first."

I told him "I promise," and now it's more than fifty years later. I've been in many different types of business deals and visited almost forty different countries. In all these transactions, I have always kept my promise to my grandfather that I would never do anything that wouldn't make "America first."

High School Secret Clubs

Yes, many of us belonged to high school fraternities, but they were not really clubs; everyone knew who the members were. However, I did know of one secret club. Before describing this "club," I must explain how important the movies and movie stars were to everyone in the 1940's.

Almost everyone went to the movies every week, and we all had favorite movie stars. Clark Gable, Alan Ladd and Tyrone Power were among the men, and among the women were Joan Crawford, Loretta

Young and Rita Hayworth. Pictures of movie stars were wherever you went. For example, if you bought an ice cream dixie cup, on the inside cover of the cup was a picture of a movie star. And for us high school boys we only hoped that it would be a picture of a beautiful movie actress. I can't tell you in this book the kind of thoughts that went through our heads as we licked off the excess ice cream from the picture on the inside of dixie cup lids.

This "Hollywood fixation" led many of us to worship one of the most beautiful woman who ever existed—Elizabeth Taylor.

All of us probably first discovered Elizabeth Taylor in the movie National Velvet. But as she grew into a beautiful woman, some of my friends (led by "Big Dave") decided what was needed was not just a fan club, but a secret society concerning Elizabeth Taylor—the Secret Elizabeth Taylor Society (code named "SETS").

Members of SETS truly believed that they could influence events in her world by deep concentration, and as SETS matured, Big Dave began having seances where we would attempt to put a hex on anyone who was dating or marrying "our" Elizabeth Taylor. The first date that was described in a movie magazine was with the famous 1940's halfback for the Army at West Point, Glen Davis (when Glen Davis and Doc Blanchard led Army to the National Football Championship). Upon reading the magazine article, Big Dave called a special meeting of SETS. At this meeting, all members sat around in a circle and with their hands laying on the table palms up and concentrated on hexing Glen Davis. And the hex worked! The next issue of the movie magazine reported that Elizabeth Taylor had broken up with Glen Davis.

All the SETS members were amazed at their hex power. But then disaster struck. The radio reported that Elizabeth Taylor had married Nicky Hilton, the heir to the Hilton Hotel chains. Big Dave called another meeting of SETS and said he realized that we hadn't done our job properly; we hadn't prevented this terrible marriage. An emotional seance was then held and a heavy hex was put on the marriage. We knew because of our power that this marriage couldn't last and it didn't. Again, the power of the hex prevailed.

This hexing continued from husband to husband; Elizabeth Taylor had married Michael Wilding, and after they were divorced she married Michael Todd (the producer of "Around the World in 80 Days"). Not only did he have the *chutzpah* of marrying our girl, but he had her convert to Judaism—he was trying to make Elizabeth into the Goddess or Queen like our Passaic high school girls were. This was totally unacceptable. Because of this hated marriage, SETS had seances every other day, with palms absolutely upright to guarantee a super hex.

As you probably know, our hex was just too strong. It probably was the reason that Michael Todd was killed when his airplane crashed. We decided we could no longer use our full powers; it was too dangerous.

Then there was Eddie Fisher, who we of course, detested. And then Richard Burton. On Richard Burton we made our hex just a little too light. Yes, they got divorced, but because the hex wasn't done right, they got remarried.

To this day I wonder if Elizabeth Taylor knows how we in Passaic High School had determined the fate of her love life.

And Speaking of Sex

Yes, I know SETS activities with Elizabeth Taylor had nothing to do with sex, but what occurred on High Street in Passaic Park did.

We guys were sitting around discussing various important issues of life. During one of these bull sessions we began discussing the subject of death. We were great philosophers. We argued why there was death, what might occur after death, would all the world's religions go to different heavens or hells. And we also discussed different types of death—slow and painful death versus instantaneous, without knowing what was happening, death. We discussed all of these subjects in gory detail.

Until finally "F" said the following, "Marilyn Monroe is the most vivacious and sensual woman ever created." (All heads nodded yes, even the members of the Secret Elizabeth Taylor Society.) F went on to say, "Thus, I would very much like to someday not only meet her but put my arm around her." We also nodded furiously wondering what the hell this had to do with death.

He then said once he had his arm around her he would slowly remove each piece of her clothing as he gently would place her into a reclining position. (We all began to drool and breathe a little bit faster.) He would then fully undress her and he would gently, but with his heart pounding fast, climb on top of her and mount her. We all sat there with our eyes wide open until some stupid guy in the group interrupted and said, "What has this got to do with death?"

"F" looked at us and then said, "When Marilyn Monroe and I would finally reach the climatic moment, the way I'd like to die is to have an elephant step on my ass."

It was unanimous among all of us. "F" had found the answer that if you have to die, could anybody every imagine a better way for it to happen?

And Speaking of Sex#2

In downtown Passaic, next to the Montauk Theater on the second floor was the Ritz Ballroom. This was without question the finest, most prestigious place where anyone could ever hold a social event. Not only was it used for the annual "Turkey Hop" sponsored by my high school fraternity, but I discovered that the competing high school fraternity of ABG was to hold, for the first time, its annual national convention in Passaic and they had rented the Ritz Ballroom for three consecutive days and nights.

The first two days were banquets and business meetings that were for ABG members only. However, the third night was called "Entertainment

Night" and they invited other high school fraternities to also attend if they would pay the one dollar admission charge.

Of course, they never explained what "entertainment" meant. However, we all eagerly paid our dollar to find out. That night finally came and all of us went up to this elegant ballroom. At the top of the wide marble stairs that we had to climb to go to the ballroom, they had placed a screen that blocked viewing the inside of the ballroom. So we paid our dollar and went into the ballroom. What we saw were about 500 other high school youths all playing craps in different areas on the floor. There were no tables, there were just crap games and people were betting various amounts, from a minimum of ten cents a roll to as high as two dollars a roll. It was truly a gigantic gambling casino.

This went on for about an hour until the owner of the Ritz Ballroom came up the stairs to see if there were any problems that he could help with (not many organizations rented the Ritz Ballroom for three consecutive days; it was a gold mine to him). When he walked around the screen and saw the gambling on the floor, he began screaming and yelling that we're all going to be arrested and we're all going to be going to jail and that the Ritz Ballroom will be closed forever, and we've got to stop.

Since the ABG people were in charge and since they were like most respectful teenagers, everyone totally ignored him and went on with the crap games. He made a frantic run around the room pleading with everybody to STOP. No one stopped. He then said he was going to go find the police before they found the gambling themselves and he went running down the stairs and out of the building.

The crap games continued for another ten minutes and then an announcement was made that we should stop. We all assumed that this was because of the possibility of the police coming. However, that was not the reason.

Suddenly, from the door of the Ritz kitchen a lady paraded into the ballroom—maybe she wasn't a lady or perhaps she was a professional lady—maybe even that's a bit too nice. She was a stripper, although, at that point in time she was totally clothed. As she pranced out of the kitchen area, a record player began playing the kind of music that we had previously heard at the Empire Burlesque Theater in Union City, New Jersey. She danced between the guys and took off her feathered shawl and then began a slow erotic strip tease act.

Now we who had worshiped Elizabeth Taylor and Marilyn Monroe realized that this stripper did not have much beauty. Moreover, she was somewhat plump. However, except for our fantasies and nighttime dreams, none of us had really ever seen a woman slowly taking off her clothes. It was most erotic.

And as she got down to the bare minimums, the Ritz's owner again showed up. You could hear frantic conversation on the other side of the screen where he was talking to the AGB official whose job was to watch out for the police. The AGB official was pleading that the owner shouldn't go into the ballroom at this time. The official kept repeating this was a bad time. It was a very poor time. It was a time for which he'd always be sorry if he went in.

This caused the owner to become even more concerned for his Ritz Ballroom. He was screaming at the ABG guard saying that he didn't go to the police because he wanted to try once again to have "the young lads" stop gambling. He then pushed his way past the guard and walked in just as the "entertainer" was removing the last piece of itty bitty clothing from her body.

The Ritz's owner stopped as if he had been hit with 10,000 volts of electricity. I could swear his eyes popped out at least six inches from his head. The veins on his head stood out, the veins on his neck stood out. It was a miracle that he survived. He then ran to where the stripper was. Before he could say anything, the stripper, who obviously had encountered this type of problem before, grabbed him and gave him the biggest wettest kiss that any of us had ever seen or imagined. He protested, but not too hard. Then the stripper as their lips parted, whispered something in his ear and a new record was put on. It was obvious that the stripper was to exit the hall to this record. The stripper kept her arm tightly around the owner and they gently and slowly moved to the kitchen area and then closed the doors.

None of us knew what happened behind that closed door, but we all vividly imagined what happened. We didn't see the owner again that night at all. We also didn't see the stripper. We went back and began to play craps, but all thoughts and all eyes remained fixed on that kitchen door.

Yes, Passaic was a great city in which to grow up!

CHAPTER 11

Graduating from PHS

A s winter turned to spring in 1950, many of my friends were busy taking the "College Boards." These were the equivalent to today's "SAT Tests" that become part of their college admissions materials. Those of us who had coasted through high school didn't bother taking the College Boards. We were going to make it in the world without any further education.

However, as the days warmed I began to become panicky, and questioned whether the decision not to go to college was intelligent. I was also jealous of Gideon who had been accepted to Cooper Union and Alan who had been accepted to the University of Illinois, and my many other friends who had been accepted to different colleges. I began to wonder what I was going to do with my life. I decided to meet with Dr. Dales, one of the two "Guidance Counselors" who were at the school. Dr. Dales, a stuffy older gentleman, suggested, and I agreed, to take a battery of "aptitude tests" on the following Saturday. These tests were designed to help direct a student to choose a career.

On Saturday, about a half dozen other "misfits" and I wandered into the school and started the tests. The tests went on for about four hours and to my great surprise I found them interesting. At the end of the last test, the monitor handed each of us an appointment card with the time that Dr. Dales would discuss the results of the tests.

At the appointed hour, I walked into Dr. Dales' office and noticed he was again seated in his typical unsmiling mood. He said that the tests showed that I had "an aptitude in mathematics" and that I might succeed in college. However, he pointed out that in high school I had a rather poor record and was near the bottom of my class. He modified this somewhat, recognizing that I had taken all the advanced College Preparatory classes and perhaps there might be some college somewhere that would accept me.

Dr. Dales suggested that he would give me a letter of recommendation and that I should also get a letter of recommendation from the head of the math department, Mr. Ruland Anderson.

He took out a yellow ruled pad and began taking notes about my extracurricular activities, organizations I belonged to, etc. When I mentioned that I was currently president of the high school fraternity AZA, he put the pencil down and looked up at me sharply. He sternly said I should never tell that to anybody because AZA was a pinko organization; a communist front organization that would attempt to overthrow the U.S. government (by 1950 the Cold War was at its height, and Senator Joseph McCarthy was at his maximum influence as a communist hunter).

I was indeed shocked that he said that AZA was a communist front. To the best of my knowledge we really never did anything except run one dance a year, and have weekly fights at our meetings. I left Dr. Dales' office somewhat puzzled but with my anger growing. That evening I described the meeting with Dr. Dales with my mother and father. My mother was a very active political person in Passaic, and one of the major sponsors of the "Cinnamon League;" an organization that supported Julius Cinnamon, one of the perennial successful politicians who ran Passaic.

My mother telephoned Cinnamon at his home and described Dr. Dales' allegation that AZA was a communist front organization. She then telephoned Morris Pashman, a powerful lawyer and city politician who was about to run for mayor of Passaic. She told him the same story.

(Historical Note: Morris Pashman had been a star basketball player on Passaic High's Wonder Teams.)

My mother also wanted to call Cousin Morris, the gangster. I pleaded with her not to call him, because the only thing our cousin would think of doing would be unlawful and painful. She finally agreed not to call him.

I never learned what Cinnamon or Pashman did that night. However, when I got to school the next morning, my home room teacher, Mrs. Card, told me that I was to immediately see Dr. Dales.

My home room (Room 107) was only about fifty feet from Dr. Dales' office in the front part of the building. During that fifty feet I prepared myself for a giant fight because I had decided to strongly defend AZA. He was not going to insult the most important organization I ever belonged to, even though it never did anything.

When I got to Dr. Dales' office he stood up (up to that point in time I didn't really know he had legs) and smiled at me. He asked if I would **mind** sitting down. I sat. He then sat down himself and continued to have a broad smile on his face.

Dr. Dales said that apparently I had misunderstood him yesterday. In no way did he mean to indicate that my high school fraternity AZA was a communist front. His only intention was to warn me to avoid any organization that might have been a communist front. My first reaction was to say baloney, and my second reaction was to say you're a damn liar.

But my actual reaction was, "Thank you for clarifying the matter." I deliberately attempted not to smile but to be stone faced.

Dr. Dales then reached into his desk and pulled out a typed letter on high school stationery. He said he stayed up the previous night and typed it himself. The letter was a very strong recommendation to the Dean of the Engineering School at New York University to accept me for the fall semester. He said he had known the Dean for many years; they had gone to high school together. He then offered to arrange an appointment for me to be interviewed by the Dean about possible admittance that fall.

I thanked him, still without a smile, but told him I was not interested in such an interview, got up, and walked out of the room.

That short meeting with Dr. Dales was a defining experience of my life. It proved to me the importance of powerful friends—whether the friends are mine or somebody else's that would intercede on my part (like my mother). It also proved to me that even the high and mighty, like Dr. Dales, kowtow to someone who is still higher and mightier than them.

*   *   *

I also received a strong letter of recommendation from Mr. Anderson, with whom I had taken all the advanced mathematics courses. But having only two letters of recommendation and being near the bottom of my high school graduating class, and without having taken the College Boards, I really didn't think it was worthwhile going to the prestigious NYU for an interview.

The last months of our high school came and went in a flash. The senior prom, the graduation ceremony, and suddenly the freedom of being finished with all public school training. However, suddenly I was faced with the crisis of what to do with the rest of my life. Would I go into business with my father and uncle in the men's store? Or what else?

*   *   *

The answer to my future was not decided by me or by my family or by the Passaic school system. It was decided by the president of North Korea.

*   *   *

On June 27, 1950, North Korea invaded South Korea across the 38th Parallel. Instantly, President Truman declared that the United States would assist South Korea in its struggle to survive. He immediately dispatched American soldiers to Korea under the command of World War II hero, General Douglas MacArthur. At the same time, the United States went to the United Nations Security Council to seek a resolution that the other United Nations countries would join with the United States to defend South Korea.

In one way, this invasion occurred at an ideal time. The Soviet Union had previously walked out of the Security Council and were boycotting it. The boycott eliminated the threat of a Soviet veto to stop the Security Council. The Security Council thus voted in favor of the "police action" which most of us called the Korean War, one of the bloodiest wars the United States was ever in.

The decision to support South Korea caused the President to announce a large increase in the drafting of civilians into the Army. Obviously, since I was of draft age, without a job, and having completed high school, I was a prime candidate to go in the Army. I really wouldn't have minded going in the Army except the thought of other people trying to shoot me was not one of my favorite daydreams. I decided I had no choice but to go to college because college students, at that time, received an automatic "2S" draft deferment.

The next day I got into my '38 Chevy, drove across the Washington Bridge and went to the NYU campus in the Bronx. I was amazed at the beauty of this forty-eight acre campus. After walking around and meeting people, I discovered that the campus housed two different colleges, Fine Arts and Engineering. They differed from NYU's downtown campus, with the Fine Arts College considered a better prerequisite for acceptance into law school and medical school, and NYU's Engineering College which was subdivided into various categories such as civil, electrical, mechanical and aeronautical engineering.

Not knowing any better, I brazenly walked into the Dean of Engineering's office and showed the receptionist the letter to him from Dr. Dales. I asked if I could see the Dean. The receptionist reluctantly took the letter to the Dean, and to her surprise, the Dean invited me right in.

I gave the Dean a transcript of my high school records and the two letters of recommendation. I told him that I had goofed off all during high school but really thought I had what it took to become an engineer.

He was a very sharp and jovial guy and appreciated that I was straightforward by handing him my poor high school transcript. He took the time to explain that engineering was a very difficult college to attend. He told me that over half the freshman class did not survive into the second year. Moreover, only one in four freshman ever graduates from NYU engineering schools.

Arrogantly I told him that I was obviously the one that would. (I kept thinking about those North Koreans getting ready to shoot me if I didn't get into NYU.) He leaned back and said, "Let's make a deal." He asked if I would agree to sign a letter stating that in order to protect NYU's reputation, I would voluntarily drop out of NYU, and not get any tuition refund, if and when the Dean would ever ask me to. My answer was quite simple, "It's a deal."

Right then and there he wrote up the letter and I signed it. He then asked what engineering school I wanted to enter.

Up to that point in time I hadn't given any thought to that question. I simply wanted to get into a college. Now on the spur of the moment I was being forced to make a lifetime decision, and yet, although I couldn't admit it to him, I didn't even know what type of work was done by an engineer. I asked him to explain what the curriculum was at the acronautical engineering school.

He explained that NYU's aeronautical engineering program was one of seven schools in the United States that were "Guggenheim Schools of Aeronautics." Others included MIT, Cal Tech and Cornell. All of these schools had been endowed by one of the benevolent nineteenth century "robber barons." Mr. Guggenheim's goal was to encourage the United States to achieve the world's leadership role in aviation. I quickly told the Dean the story of having seen the Hindenburg as a very young child, and having been at Teeterboro when the first DC-3 landed there, and having built model airplanes during the war effort. While talking, my mind was making the decision, and I finally said, "Yes, I want to go to NYU's Guggenheim School of Aeronautics."

Of course, there were still some minor problems to overcome. First of all I had to tell my parents that I was going to go to college. I knew that they would approve. The second thing I'd have to tell my parents is that they would have to pay for me to go to college. That answer was less certain. And the third thing I had to tell my parents was that they had to pay for me to go to college at the most expensive school in the United States, NYU. One semester's tuition at NYU was an astounding $470.

When I announced that number to my father, he shuddered a bit, and then smiled and said, "Go, but be successful." He then added that he would pay for the tuition and the books, however, it would be up to me to earn enough money to commute to NYU from Passaic (about an hour commute by car), and any other money I needed except for an allowance of $5 a week.

For the second time that day, I said, "It's a deal!"

*   *   *

I immediately began planning how to get the commuting money. I knew that an older friend from Passaic, Marty Willinski, was already going to NYU's Aeronautical Engineering School. He had lived down the street from me, and was a leader in the Boy Scout Troop that I had belonged to. Moreover, Marty didn't have a car and he was anxiously seeking someone to drive him. I called Marty up and immediately made a deal with him. I would charge him $10 a week for the daily round-trip ride to NYU.

Marty's $10 was more than one third of the money I needed to operate my car. I had estimated it would cost $25 a week to commute.

Of this $2.50 would be for tolls for the Washington Bridge—twenty five cents each way when you bought a Commuter Book—$12 for gas (driving 80 miles each day with a car getting ten miles per gallon, and gas costing about 30 cents per gallon), money for car repairs, and the rest for many quarts of oil.

My car, which we all called Penelope, had a few minor problems. The muffler had a large hole in it so the exhaust fumes bellowed under the car. In addition, there were large holes in the floor of the car so that the fumes were able to get into the car. In the winter the holes also let freezing air rush into the car. But the major problem was that Penelope burnt plenty of oil—two quarts of oil each way in the forty mile trip to NYU. And oil cost about forty cents a quart, too expensive for my commuting budget.

But Penelope's old age allowed a unique solution to the oil cost problem; I used oil that didn't cost me anything. The free oil was drained out of other cars during oil changes. Of course, the oil was filthy but I took care of that by pouring the oil through a piece of cheesecloth. This captured many large dirt particles but obviously, the oil was still rather filthy.

I rationalized that this dirty oil was good for the car because it had more particles to get stuck in the worn piston rings that were allowing oil to slosh through it. Thus, every morning before driving to school I would pour two quarts of oil in, and every day when I left NYU, another two quarts went in.

Everybody could always see us coming. There was this big blue smoke cloud that hovered over Penelope at all times. It was beautiful. (This was before the days when people worried about air pollution.)

But I still had to fill two more seats of my car before I could afford to commute to NYU. I then remembered that my cousin, Marilyn, had enrolled in a bi-lingual school that was located in downtown New York. A quick phone call, and quick agreement; she would drive to the Bronx in the car pool, and then take the subway to downtown New York. She agreed to pay $5/week since she would have to take the bus home.

Then I discovered that one of my more popular classmates, Phil Epstein, had enrolled at NYU's Fine Arts College. A quick meeting, a quick agreement, and the last needed $10/week was secured.

*   *   *

Yes, the summer of 1950 was most eventful—graduating from high school, the newspaper filled with terrifying stories of the war in Korea, the local draft board chasing all of my friends, acceptance to NYU, and creating the paying car pool. And to top off all these events, I even convinced my friend Moishe to transfer from his New Jersey college to NYU, thus, providing an extra $10 per week.

All of these events provided a meaningful closure to those wonderful years of growing up and being educated in my beloved City of Passaic.

PART 3

Passaic Is Always With You

CHAPTER 12

Moving From Passaic

Yes, I graduated with the Class of 1950, which although I'm a little prejudiced, was probably the finest graduating class in the history of Passaic High School. In 1954 I graduated from NYU as an aeronautical engineer.

During the entire four years in college I was dating a girl from the nearby, much more affluent city of Teaneck, New Jersey. I had met her during the summer of 1950 and we became inseparable, and finally our wedding was planned for Easter break in my senior year of college. It has now been forty-six years since Carole and I married (fifty years since we met) and not only is she my wife, she's also my closest friend, and business partner.

Often I have been asked the question did I ever think of divorcing Carole during these forty-six years of marriage. I can truthfully say the thought never crossed my mind. However, if I must be perfectly honest, I would also say that although divorce didn't cross my mind, murder certainly did, many times!

But that may be true with most married people.

As our wedding plans were finalized in 1954, I hoped I would be able to obtain a job with the Curtis Wright Company, one of America's leading manufacturers of airplane engines. It was a direct descendant from the company started by Orville Wright who invented the airplane. The Curtis Wright Company was located in a city just a few miles from Passaic.

Carole and I began to hunt for a place to live. As luck would have it, in the two family house in which my friend Phil Epstein lived, the upstairs apartment became available. Carole and I went to look at it and it looked ideal to us. It was recently modernized and was on Prospect Street only one block from downtown Passaic. Thus, we invited my future mother-in-law, Mrs. Spector, to visit the apartment. (For reader clarity, I will call her by her first name, "Minnie").

To say the very least, Minnie was the central person in her entire very large extended family. Almost every Sunday the entire family from New York, New Jersey and elsewhere would meet at her house in Teaneck where they would entertain themselves with the various typical family arguments and eat Minnie's food and really enjoy themselves.

It was on a Sunday morning before one of these family get-togethers that Carole and I drove Minnie to see the apartment. She walked upstairs in this old building, took one look at the apartment, turned around and walked out and sat in the car. Carole and I looked at each other and finally we returned to the car. As we opened the door, Minnie stated, "No daughter of mine will live in such an apartment." Carole didn't know what to say because she was torn between being nice to her mother or defending her fiancé. I didn't say a word.

We drove back to Teaneck in total silence. When we got to Carole's house she became very busy as the company began arriving. This house had a very large living room and everybody tended to sit around the living room chatting, discussing and arguing about the events of the past week. In mid-afternoon I got up and walked out to my car, opened the glove compartment, took out a large group of letters and a map of the United States. Returning to the house, I went to the kitchen drawer and got a ball of string, a pair of scissors and many straight pins, which I carried into the living room.

Without saying a word to anybody I laid down on the floor and spread out the map of the United States. Someone asked what I was doing but I didn't answer (I hadn't said anything since the morning incident). I first put a pin in the map locating Teaneck, New Jersey. I took the packet of letters which were the thirteen different job offers I had received during my job interviews. I opened each letter, looked at the return address and stuck a pin into the map where that company was located. I then tied a piece of string from the Teaneck pin to that company's pin location.

Now everybody was watching me. I commenced to do this for all thirteen companies for which I had job offers. Of course, the shortest string was to Curtis-Wright which on the map was only about an eighth inch long. I also had job offers in St. Louis, Columbus, Seattle, Texas and several different locations in California. In a little while the map was covered with strings, each of them a different length. When I finally completed installing all the strings, there was no other conversation in the room. Everybody simply looked at the map. At that instant I got up, walked to the kitchen, opened the closet, took out the yard stick and walked back to the map. Carefully I then measured the lengths of all the strings. I found that the string from Teaneck to Santa Monica, California, was the longest string. I picked up the letter from the Douglas Aircraft Company in Santa Monica, walked over to the telephone, dialed the operator and placed a call to the Douglas Aircraft Company, reversing the charges. No one among the relatives had probably ever made a long-distance call to California, and thus they watched in awe.

I told whoever answered the phone that I was accepting their job offer and would start the first week in June, approximately eight weeks from the date of the call.

When I got off the phone my fiancé came over to me and smiled (one other possibility I thought of was that she might kill me) and she told me she was looking forward to moving to California. All the other relatives stared at me as if I had suddenly disappeared from the human race. At that instant I turned to Minnie and I said, "I agree with you.

Your daughter will never live in that apartment on Prospect Street in Passaic. By the way, what's for dinner?"

*   *   *

Being an engineer in the defense industry is a lot like being a gypsy. You tend to move quite a bit, depending upon the ebb and flow of business in the industry. In 1956, two years after joining Douglas, the company was booming and they opened up a facility in Tulsa, Oklahoma, to which they transferred me. We lived there for a few years, then we would move to the Grumman Company on Long Island, and five years later to Maryland.

*   *   *

Next to Passaic, the city I loved best was Tulsa, Oklahoma. The reason was the unique characteristic of Oklahoma in the 1950's. The state did not allow the sale of liquor or beer (prohibition reigned)! So instead of legal sales, everyone had their own bootlegger and the public was very happy with this arrangement. It provided home delivery and there was enough competition to keep the prices very reasonable. Moreover, since liquor was illegal there was no state liquor tax which also helped to keep the price very inexpensive.

The lack of legal liquor sales meant that there were very few first class restaurants. This meant that the movies would end early and there weren't very many places to go. This lack of night life was more than made up by the close friendships that quickly developed in Tulsa. Without exterior clubs, movies and other things to go to, entertaining at home was warm and wonderful. For example, every Sunday afternoon you either stayed at home and then you would have five to twenty friends drop in unannounced, or you would drive around the city and drop into different friends' homes. If you were out cruising the city, and people came to your house, they would leave personal cards indicating

· 126 ·

that they had come to visit you. Thus, the next time you went out cruising you would make a point to visit them.

Extremely close friendships evolved. For example, about ten years after leaving Tulsa, my wife and I and our four boys made a special trip to Tulsa to visit our friends who we hadn't seen since we moved away.

Upon our arrival in Tulsa one of our friends hosted a large party where we were the guests of honor. In the large crowd, there was one man who appeared very familiar and yet he didn't speak with the Midwest type of accent. He spoke with a New Jersey accent. When I had a chance to talk to him he mentioned that he remembered me from Passaic. He said he lived in Paterson and hung out at the Paterson "Y" where the Passaic guys would sometimes go. Moreover, his Paterson "Y" guys would sometimes go to the Passaic "Y" where I hung out.

Yes, I clearly remembered him and I clearly remembered the great fight we once had between the Passaic Y and the Paterson Y. And of course, any great fight was caused by GIRLS.

He then asked if I was still friendly with the "Giant Spinner." I knew immediately who he as talking about.

Jay Alexander was one of my close high school classmates who also hung out at the Passaic Y. Jay was about 6'2", and had a not quite athletic shape, but was very strong. Well, in the 1950's, fights didn't involve knives or guns. Fights involved fists. Moreover we at the Passaic Y—if I would dare admit it—were "chickens." We didn't like the thought of fighting because we might get hurt. Therefore, we devised a secret weapon.

Before describing the weapon let me describe another one of my good friends, Charlie. Charlie was a skinny guy like me, but, he was much braver than I was (for example, he enlisted in the Army paratroopers during the Korean war). Maybe the word "brave" is the wrong word. Maybe a word like fearless or crazy would be better. And thus our Y had a "big Jay," and "small, light and brave, and maybe crazy, Charlie."

That combination became our secret weapon.

I clearly remember the evening when the Paterson guys showed up at the Passaic Y hunting girls in Passaic. We took great offense and right in front of the Y on Jefferson Street (which is now where the new police station is—isn't that ironic) the fight ensued. There were about six of them and six of us. But one of the six of us was me who tended to hide behind anything that would protect me.

As soon as the fight started we released our secret weapon. Jay picked Charlie up by his ankles and began spinning him in bigger and bigger circles. Anybody from Paterson that got in the way was mowed down by being hit by Charlie's head. It was devastating. The Paterson guys retreated in panic, jumped in their cars and went home.

Yes, I certainly remembered the Giant Spinner.

This conversation with the ex-Paterson man at the Tulsa party turned out to be a startling event of my life. He mentioned to me that on Saturday nights, the Paterson guys would get in their cars and drive to the Passaic Y. I asked him the obvious question, "Why would they do that." He gave me an astonishing answer. "Because the Passaic girls were easy!"

I was astonished. I had lived my whole life in Passaic and never found an easy Passaic girl. In fact, as I told him, on Saturday night all of us Passaic guys would jump into our cars and drive to the Paterson Y because the Paterson girls were easy!

He looked at me in astonishment saying he never was able to get a date with a Paterson girl. I looked at him in astonishment and said I never had a date with a Passaic girl.

We both realized that the old proverb is really true. The grass is greener on the other side of the street—or the girls are easier in adjacent cities when they don't know you from childhood.

CHAPTER 13

To the Moon! Courtesy of Passaic

In 1958 the Soviets launched the first space satellite, Sputnik. They quickly followed it up by launching a dog into space.

Everyone in the United States was frightened by these Soviet triumphs. Did these triumphs mean that the Soviets could now launch heavy missiles with nuclear weapons against America? Did it mean that America was no longer the greatest technological country in the world? Does it mean that the communists were going to win the world?

Several months after Sputnik, the United States finally launched its first satellite under the direction of the former German scientist Wernher von Braun, who was located in Huntsville, Alabama. Even this success didn't ease the fear of the Soviet Union that gripped most Americans.

Very few people realized that there was no need to panic, that the United States had a secret weapon. That secret weapon was again Jay Alexander.

Before discussing the secret weapon, some more history is required. President Kennedy made his famous speech in 1961 where he pledged that America would send a man to the moon and back in the 60's decade. This started a major national effort under the direction of NASA to achieve this spectacular goal. Part of this effort required building the largest rocket ever conceived—the Saturn-V. The man in charge of design and building the Saturn-V was the same Wernher von Braun who launched America's first unmanned satellite.

The Saturn-V was an enormous three-stage rocket. To be able to carry the weight of the Apollo Spacecraft to the moon, it required that the third rocket stage—called the S-IVB stage—be extremely light. Any extra weight in that stage meant less weight available for the Apollo manned spacecraft.

In 1962 NASA sent out a request for proposals to the aerospace industry for the design of the S-IVB stage. At that time I was an engineer at the Grumman Corporation on Long Island and was part of a team that submitted a bid. We proposed a unique extremely light weight, thin metal design—what we called an "eggshell design"—for this large rocket.

It ended up that Grumman was one of three finalists in the competition and the great Wernher von Braun, and his entire entourage from Huntsville, came to Grumman to see our proposal and to discuss it. We at Grumman scurried to clean up the rather dingy facility and to make a model of our design.

When von Braun finally arrived and reviewed the proposal, he acknowledged that the Grumman design was the lightest he had ever seen. He asked where the concept for this "eggshell design" was researched and developed. All heads turned to me and I answered, "It was developed and proven during my junior year in high school by my friend, Jay Alexander." Von Braun looked surprised and shocked. He asked what type of test facility did we use? I answered somewhat shakily, "The toilet bowl in his house."

Yes, Jay Alexander was one of my good friends. And he was a lousy poker player! Jay's unique combination of being both physically strong and a lousy poker led to the success of the Apollo Program. Let me explain.

Our high school "gang" included about forty guys, which meant that at any single time we could host almost eight poker games, and playing poker was very important to us. As I remember, it was a cool fall evening when Jay informed us at the Y that his folks were out for the evening and we could come over to his house for a poker game. Since playing poker was the second most fun in our lives (the first, of course, thinking about how we would make conquests with girls), off we went, six of us, to Jay's house. Jay, as a gracious host, found a filthy deck of playing cards and we played on his kitchen table (no one had a dining room in those days). The game was fierce and the stakes were high, nickel and dime, which in those days was quite high.

The game proceeded in the usual fashion. Jay was losing, and unfortunately, I was also losing. In fact, I had lost almost a dollar, an astronomical sum considering that none of us had a job at that time.

It was then that I had this brilliant thought of how to make Jay reimburse my losses. I turned to Jay and said, "You know Jay, you really aren't as strong as you look. In fact, I think you're a weakling." Jay responded calmly, "What the hell are you talking about?" I said, "Jay, in fact, I'm willing to bet you a dollar you can't squash a fresh egg in one hand."

The murmur of excitement raced around the poker table. Everybody turned to Jay and Jay looked at me and said, "You must be crazy! Certainly, I can squash an egg in my fist." He bit on my bait and I had to carefully reel him in.

I carefully explained the rules. He was to put the egg in his strongest hand and he'd have to press the egg only from its top and bottom; he could not press the circumference of the egg.

Jay gave me his famous smirk which indicated that he had supreme confidence and then made the basic statement, "Put up your dollar or shut up." Luckily, I did have one more dollar and placed it on the table. Jay reached into his wallet and pulled out a dollar and matched it.

The other poker players watched this in astonishment and thought I was crazy. After all, Jay was the biggest and strongest guy of this motley group. I just sat there with a serene smile on my face.

Jay went to the refrigerator and got an egg. I then took a soft pencil and marked the two "poles" of the egg where Jay was allowed to squeeze against so that he would not squeeze on the circumference, the equator of the egg.

Jay then said we couldn't do this in the kitchen because when the egg squashed it would splatter all over the kitchen and that would get him into deep trouble. We thus decided that the place to do it was with Jay's hand reaching into the toilet bowl. Off we went, all six of us crowding into this tiny old-fashioned bathroom with Jay being the biggest guy using up most of the room. The moment arrived. Jay placed his hand half way down the toilet with pressure on the two "poles" at the ends of the egg, and squeezed with all his might. Nothing happened.

Jay glared at me and said he knew the trick. It's because by him leaning over, it didn't allow enough strength in his hand in order to squeeze the egg. I just smiled at him and said, "I'll give you one more chance and then I'm going into the kitchen and pick up the money."

Jay got on his knees, his face totally filled with determination. He lowered his hand into the top of the toilet bowl. He clenched his teeth. He gave a mighty grunt and squeezed with all his might, and

Nothing happened for about five seconds. And then...

The argument was enormous. I yelled that Jay began to squeeze on the equator of the egg and the egg squashed and broke and splattered all over, including all over Jay. I told Jay he had violated the rules and I was taking the money. Of the other four witnesses, two of them agreed with me, and two of them were Jay's close friends who, of course, lied for him.

A mad dash for the kitchen occurred at that point between the various teams of witnesses. I being the skinniest and the smallest made it out the door first and got to the kitchen table, grabbed the money and ran out the front door.

My last sight of Jay, over my shoulder, was of him standing there with his hand and face dripping from squashed egg. He had a strange look on his face as if in a trance. Perhaps he was seeing twelve years in the future.

"Yes, Dr. von Braun, the way we tested the shell theory was in Jay Alexander's toilet. He proved that as long as you don't put any force on the equator of a shell and only on the ends of a shell, it can survive enormous loads."

Von Braun nodded and the rest is really history. The S-IVB stage used the shell theory and it worked beautifully, and Apollo 12 landed on the moon, having been propelled to the moon and back by the S-IVB rocket.

Yes, America has a lot to thank Jay for, and of course, I might even thank him some day for the dollar that I conned him out of.

Commentary

After college, Jay became a pharmacist and a successful business man. I can only hope he had learned his lesson, and doesn't play poker any longer.

CHAPTER 14

Passaic Handwriting

In the spring of 1982, I was in a small city in China about a hundred miles west of Beijing. Even though the Cultural Revolution was officially over, the remnants of it still existed, and therefore, it was a bit dangerous for westerners to be in this part of China. For that reason the Chinese government provided three People's Liberation Army soldiers to accompany me everywhere. On my final day, I went to the lobby of the decrepit, filthy hotel to wait for some form of transportation to take me back to Beijing. While sitting in the lobby, I was writing a letter to my wife and I noticed another westerner enter the lobby and sit on the only other chair that was available (the one right next to me).

It was rather nice seeing another westerner, and I was hoping that he could speak English. To my great delight, I found that he had a New York area accent and after some questioning, found he currently lived in Pittsburgh, Pennsylvania.

He glanced down at the letter I was writing and perked up his head and said, "Are you originally from Passaic, New Jersey?" This of course, startled me, but when I looked down at the letter I realized how he knew. He must have also been, at some time or other, a student in the Passaic school system in the 1940's.

Those who went to school in Passaic in the late 30's through the 40's, were involved in a twenty-year experiment on teaching better penmanship. This experiment involved not teaching students how to write "script" (cursive); instead we were only taught how to print clearly and effectively.

Unfortunately, during this experiment other kids moved into Passaic who had been taught script, and thus, they were able to take notes much faster than we "printers." This caused the Passaic students to become separated into three different categories: the minority that knew script because they had come in from outside schools; those kids that printed beautifully (oh, how I was jealous of Anita Marguglio and Carol Salerno, who epitomized this group), and those that learned to scribble in order to try to keep up with their note taking (of whom I was perhaps the worst scribbler).

But I also had another major defect in my character besides unintelligible writing—I couldn't spell worth a damn. In fact, in my 1950 high school yearbook, The Echo, the most frequent comment of my classmates when they signed it was, "To the worst speller in PHS."

Less than twelve years after graduating high school, these defects in my written abilities caused a dreadful incident to occur directly in front of President John F. Kennedy.

Yes, the Soviets had beaten the United States first into space in 1957 with Sputnik, and then they totally shocked America by launching Yuri Gagorin into orbit—the first manned orbital flight.

America was far behind. Our Mercury manned space program, designed to put a single man into orbit, was far behind schedule and the only "success" we had was a fifteen minute ride that Alan Shepherd made on top of Mercury I.

The country was frightened and President Kennedy was under enormous pressure. Not only was the Soviet Union suddenly demonstrating giant launch vehicles that could rain hydrogen bombs on U.S. cities, but the President was to blame for the recent disastrous Bay Of Pigs invasion of Cuba. Thus, the President was looking for a way to regain the public's confidence in him, and for America to demonstrate technological supremacy compared the Soviet Union.

The President directed the new government agency, named the National Air and Space Administration ("NASA"), to study possible methods of speeding up our space program. They were to study several alternate goals; for example, building an earth space station, the possibility of manned flight to the moon, experiments involving Mars, etc. The President had ordered that NASA come up with a dramatic and meaningful recommendation.

Kennedy also challenged the National Space Counsel, which was headed by Vice President Lyndon Johnson, to make a dramatic recommendation. As part of these secret studies on how to catch up with the Soviet Union, Kennedy also called for a small conference in the White House where defense industry leaders would make presentations on what type of space program they would recommend.

Unlike the usual kind of "presidential commissions" that have months to prepare, these were emergency times. The American people wanted action and President Kennedy wanted action. Therefore, the White House meeting was called with only three days' notice. One of the people invited to the meeting was the Vice President of Engineering of the Grumman Company, the company for which I was working.

I had a very responsible job at the Grumman Company. My title was "Manager of Lunar Exploration." Grumman had no contracts that had anything to do with the moon, and of course, I had nobody working for me. Moreover, I didn't even have an office; I was just one of thousands of engineers in an open "ball field." But I did have that title, which in the defense industry, means perhaps more than anything else. Why? Because if you have the title they assume you know something.

Of course, Grumman, being a very large company, was full of bureaucracy. For example, the invitation to the White House meeting that would take place in three days took two days in Grumman's interplant mail system to get to the V.P.'s office. He was left with only six hours to get ready to make a speech to the President of the United States on Grumman's recommendation.

The V.P. immediately called a meeting of all the Grumman space exploration experts (we had four people) including the "Manager of

Lunar Explanation," me. None of us had any knowledge of why he called us in until we sat down in his office. He then read us the invitation. We were all in awe that this man, who we considered a pretty good administrator but out of touch with modern engineering, was going to present Grumman's recommendation to John F. Kennedy on whether to build a manned space station, or go to Mars, or go to the moon. And he was going to the White House meeting in only a few hours.

The V.P. then asked each of the other three attendees to describe rational arguments on why the United States should immediately start building an earth orbiting manned space station. Their arguments made excellent engineering and economic sense—perhaps their strongest argument was that U.S. industry could achieve it and do it on a grand scale. However, I was Manager of Lunar Exploration, and thus, the V.P. told me to present valid arguments on why Americans should send man to the moon.

Remember, we had no notice of this meeting, and everything was done extemporaneously. However, since I had been brought up in Passaic, and in high school I had been voted "most talkative," I could shoot the bull along with the best of them.

When it came my time to speak I stood up and gave a twenty minute talk on why it was feasible to go to the moon and why it was important to go to the moon. In the feasibility section I described what I had read in the open literature, none of it very revolutionary. As for the reason to send a manned space craft to the moon, I gave a passionate speech that there would be nothing more exciting in the history of the human race than finding life on an extra terrestrial body like the moon. I ended my talk with an impassioned plea emphasizing that we should go to the moon for "the possibility of discovering extra terrestrial life—for the joy of achieving extra terrestrial organisms."

As I sat down I could see in everyone's face that I had really impressed them, and in fact the V.P. pointed at me and said, "That's the thing I want to take to the president." I puffed up my chest. (Of course, he didn't know my name, and therefore, he had to point to me, but that's a different story.)

He said, "I have to leave here in less than an hour and fly to Washington. Quickly write down what you said, and I'll use it as my notes when I give the speech to the President."

There I was in the V.P.'s conference room with his lined yellow pad writing—with my crummy Passaic printing and my crummy spelling—the speech. At that time I never felt more embarrassed nor more upset about the Passaic school system. Suddenly the V.P. rushed in and asked if I was done. Not waiting for an answer he grabbed my yellow pad and off he went on the company's private airplane to Washington, D.C.

The next morning I got a call from the V.P.'s secretary saying I was urgently needed in the V.P.'s Conference Room. When I got there, there were a number of people including the dreaded personnel people and others. We sat around and waited and then the V.P. walked in and looked at me with a strange look. I couldn't tell whether it was complimentary or hatred. He started briefing the group on what happened yesterday at the White House. He said that by the luck of the draw he was the last one to give the presentation. The first presenter was the chief engineer of the Boeing Company, then the Chief engineer of Northrop. There were a total of six presentations prior to his. He said President Kennedy listened politely to each presentation, but made no comments.

The V.P. stopped, glared at me and then started speaking again.

He said that he then made a strong presentation on why we should go to the moon. He said although he had trouble reading the handwriting (oh my God! Passaic did it to me again) and because the spelling was atrocious (oy vey!) he stumbled a few times, however he stated he did manage to bring enthusiasm to his voice when he got to the final conclusion which he carefully read as I had apparently written it.

He stated the White House audience was spellbound when he said, "We must go to the moon for the possibility of discovering if there is extra terrestrial life—for the joy of achieving extra terrestrial **orgasms**."

Everyone in our V.P.'s Conference Room broke into hysterical laughter. The V.P. even had a little smirk on his face. He said that was the exact response he got at the White House at the end of his speech.

He then passed around my handwritten scribbles to show that it was my writing that caused him to say "that word", instead of organisms.

He then said the laughter at the White House was led by President Kennedy who said to the entire assembled group, "At last I think we found a good reason why we should go to the moon." Then the V.P. said the White House conference again broke down into hysterical laughter. The V.P. said he attempted to apologize to the president saying one of his very young engineers wrote these notes and either had misspelled the word or had deliberately set up a trap for him. The President turned to him and said, "Please give my regards to that young engineer. Apparently he thinks the way I do." Again, the White House broke into laughter.

The V.P. walked out of the Grumman Conference Room. Everybody turned to look at me. I didn't know what to say. I didn't know if I was being fired. I didn't know what to do. The only thing that came to my mind was the old Passaic High School football fight song which started, "Hang Jeff Davis by the sour apple tree, down with McGinty to the bottom of the sea…"

P.S.: They gave me a round of applause and a meaningful pay raise.

*   *   *

About a year later, I resigned from Grumman and became head of Fairchild's Space Division located in Washington, D.C. As part of my job I was obligated to go to the many political and other functions that occur almost nightly in our nation's capitol.

One of these is the yearly black tie affair sponsored by the White House reporters and broadcasters. This is an off the record evening where various skits and speeches are made, usually targeting the president. At the end of the evening the president usually takes the podium and tells humorous anecdotes concerning the press.

As is customary in the defense industry, I had invited some congressmen and one senator to sit at our table (that's called lobbying) and one of my guests was an influential congressman from Texas, with whom I've had a lot of prior dealings.

The night was truly hilarious and perhaps the highlight of the night was when President Kennedy took the podium. As part of his "shtik", the President ridiculed the press about many matters. One of them was an hysterically funny description of a meeting that the President had the previous year which the press never found out about. Kennedy then described how bad penmanship had caused a distinguished industry representative to advise him, "We should go to the moon to achieve extra terrestrial **orgasms**."

The crowd went into hysterics. I cringed in my chair. The Texas congressman leaned over to me and said, "Hell, your handwriting is probably as bad as the guy that caused the orgasm remark to President Kennedy."

Yes, Miss Miscowski, (my second grade teacher at Number 11 School), you were right in saying: "Robert, you must practice your printing and learn your spelling words. If you don't, someday you will be very sorry."

CHAPTER 15

Ying Yang on a Skewer

T he following horrifying events occurred during the early morning
of Sunday, August 7, 1994 on the Severn River off the Chesapeake
Bay in Maryland. However, they are really a direct continuation of what
happened to me at Passaic General Hospital in 1947.

It Was a Dark and Stormy Night

No, it wasn't, actually it was a gorgeous night! The hot weather had
ended and it was a gorgeous August weekend.

Early in the day, my son Todd and his wife Kay, had taken our new
boat, "Dream Beam", for a pleasant day of cruising on the Chesapeake
Bay and finally ended up in Annapolis. All the moorings in Annapolis
were taken, so they dropped anchor at the foot of the Severn River just
outside the Annapolis harbor entrance. This location is next to the
practice fields of the U.S. Naval Academy.

My wife Carole, I, and Todd and Kay's two young children took a
water taxi and boarded the boat about 8:00 p.m. We noted that there
were many other boats anchored in the same area, and although it was a
little crowded, the seas were very calm. We all finally bedded down for
the night at approximately 10:30 p.m.

The Bump in the Night

Before discussing the horror that occurred, let me first mention that part of this whole horror story occurred because the manager of a small Chinese company located in Guangzhou (formerly Canton), China, decided to save one third of a penny on the manufacturing cost of pajamas. This particular factory had contracted with an American company for delivering men's pajamas. The manager had discovered that he could buy waistband elastic that was not fully cured and save one third of a penny. This partially cured elastic worked quite well until the pajamas were washed a few times in hot water. After such washings the elastic stopped being elastic, but that wasn't his problem—he had already sold the pajamas to the U.S. company.

Now back to the story.

So there we were sleeping, me in my pajamas that had worn-out elastic in the waistband. That was not really a problem because when I walked I would simply hold the pajamas up with my left hand.

Most boat owners sleep lightly, being easily awakened if something unusual occurs. Although I was asleep I felt the boat bobbing. Then it occurred.

I distinctly heard a scrape and then a bump. I leaped out of my bed, raced through the cabin, carefully holding my pajamas up with my left hand, and ran outside onto the deck. The first thing I noticed was that the wind had picked up significantly. Behind us, on the rock jetty around the Naval Academy's football practice field, there were major waves crashing. The second thing I noticed was that a sailboat, maybe 35 or 40 feet long, was about to strike the forward part of Dream Beam.

Staying calm, I did several things in rapid succession. First, I screamed at the top of my lungs for the rest of the family to awake and help avoid the impending disaster. Second, I reached over the rail to fend off (i.e. push off) the sailboat to try to protect the hull on my boat.

Now let me explain: My boat weighs about 50,000 pounds. The sailboat weighs maybe 10,000 pounds. There is a strong wind. There is no possible way to push it off with one hand. Obviously, I had to use two hands.

Just as obvious, the cheap factory manager in China could care less that by using two hands, my pajamas fell to my ankles. I feverishly reached over the railing (in the forward part of the boat there is a stainless steel railing) to fend off the sailboat.

To understand what happened next, I must explain the design of a boat railing.

The height of the boat railing is deliberately designed to try to protect people from falling overboard. The height is usually selected so that the average man and woman would both have some protection.

Since I'm only 5'7", this cold stainless steel railing came up to a position approximately half way between my upper thighs and my waist; thus, as I leaned over this cold railing, my—being from the Passaic High Class of 1950 I cannot use frank and plain language; I will call the two parts of the male anatomy the "ying and yang"—my ying and my yang both rested against this cold steel railing. Certainly the sensation of the cold railing gave a rude shock to my body. However, I was able to continue fending off the sailboat.

At that point I realized that either my boat or that sailboat had "dragged the anchor." In other words, one of the two boats was free. The sailboat in relation to my boat kept moving aft and I kept attempting to also move aft.

Unfortunately, with the pajamas wrapped around my ankles the only way I could move was to hop. Now please recognize it is uncomfortable to have your ying yang on a cold metal railing. But it is infinitely more uncomfortable to have to hop and have your ying yang banging against a cold metal railing.

Now I have to describe my boat. It is a trawler and trawlers have a lot of teak wood. In fact, the design of the boat railing uses stainless steel on the front third of the boat and then the railing changes to teak.

Therefore, as I hopped towards the center of the boat, I immediately recognized that the cold searing pain on my ying yang had stopped. I was now resting my anatomy on the warmer teak railing as I fended off the sailboat. I also had learned, instead of hopping with the pajamas around my ankles, I could slowly slide my feet. I continued to slowly slide towards the rear of my boat fending off the sailboat. I certainly was thankful that there was no longer the metal rail that my ying yang was resting on, only teakwood—wood?—suddenly my mind exploded the word S-P-L-I-N-T-E-R-S!!!

Adolescence: Thank God I Don't have to go Through That Again

I apologize for interrupting this story, however, I must provide some background so you understand my fright.

The year was 1947. I was fifteen years old and had just returned from Boy Scout Camp. Upon returning home from camp I discovered I had a terrible case of poison ivy. Moreover, the poison ivy was concentrated on my ying yang.

Of course, I would never tell my mother or father about this. However, within two or three days the case became so bad that I couldn't even go to the bathroom. Thus, I had to tell my mother, who immediately took me to Passaic General Hospital's emergency room.

My mother sat in the waiting room (God forbid a mother should see her fifteen year old son without his pants on) and the nurse took me into the doctor's office. As I recall, the nurse was young, pretty and to use the vernacular of the 1940's, she was "well stacked." (Please notice that even in my pain and agony of the poison ivy, I was able to keep my mind on the important things.)

The nurse told me that the doctor would be in shortly and I should undress. She gave me one of those hospital gowns that I didn't quite know whether to put on frontwards or backwards but it didn't make any difference. When the nurse left the room I quickly undressed, put on the hospital gown and sat on the edge of the examining table.

The doctor came in with the nurse and they carefully examined me (I was never more embarrassed, except five minutes later, than this moment). The doctor gave some instructions to the nurse and left.

Now here I was, essentially naked in a room with this "well stacked" nurse. Moreover, I was in horrible agony from the itch and the attributes of the poison ivy. The nurse, probably suspecting that I was uncomfortable, left the room putting my mind more at ease.

She then returned with two very young female nurses (oh my God, it's going to be a horror). The two other nurses (were they nurses or were they candy stripers?) also had to carefully examine my severe case of poison ivy. I cringed with embarrassment.

Then the first nurse got some medication and a cotton pad and began gently stroking the medication over all parts of my ying yang. As she did it, please forgive me, but I was only a fifteen year old adolescent, and had no control over my hormones, I began to feel this strange sensation. When the candy stripers began to giggle, I realized to my horror that little things were becoming not so little. I was mortified, horrified, and as they giggled more, the nurse began to rub the medication on using rapid short strokes. The pain became unbearable, then suddenly it turned into ecstasy and I totally lost control.

On that day I swore I would never again be put into such a humiliating situation.

And Splinters?

Running through my head was my adolescent experience of the hospital emergency room. I would not allow that to happen again even if a giant splinter were to intersect my ying yang becoming "ying yang on a skewer" or a "kabob" (notice how I got my first name in that last word).

Fortunately, there were no splinters. Also, fortunately, I managed to keep my footing. And even more fortunately, I was now about two thirds the way back on the boat, still fending off the sail boat.

About this time the rest of the crew was springing into action. My wife, Carole, was going through our trained emergency procedure. One part of that procedure is to have her open all the doors to the main cabin to allow people to get out in case we had to leave the boat.

Let me explain a little bit about Carole. She's only 5'2". She exercises twice a year; i.e. when the local department store has a big sale she pushes her way through the crowds. Otherwise, she's a lot like me, just a middle aged couch potato.

However, her adrenalin was pumping. Instead of simply sliding open each of the cabin doors (each door weighs fifty pounds), she grabbed each door with such force she lifted them out of the track and carried them and put them down on the deck—not just one door—but both doors! She was an Adrenalin Amazon!

At the same moment Todd emerged, a little sleepy but ready to help fend off. The first thing he noticed was the pajamas around my ankles which, since I was the captain, he didn't understand if this was a command for everybody to drop their pajamas. When I saw his quizzicle look, and noticed his eyes staring down at my pajamas, I calmly screamed at the top of my lungs that he should fend off the sailboat while I start our boat's engines.

During the same panic period Kay had her two children get dressed in case the sailboat would cause damage below the water line.

As Todd took over fending off the sailboat, I grabbed the pajamas, yanked them up with my left hand and began running to start the engines. Thank goodness the engines started right up. I then left the lower station and ran to the flying bridge so I could get some visibility on what was going on.

A quick glance indicated a chaotic situation in this large boat anchorage. Boats were moving on their own in all directions. On our starboard (right) side an unmanned 25 foot power launch was moving towards us. Todd was fending off the sailboat which was now near the aft part of our boat. Ahead of us a 30 foot cabin cruiser appeared to be directly aimed for a collision with the nose of our boat. There were perhaps 40 boats at this anchorage and I quickly estimated almost ten of them were floating free.

The other thing that stunned me was that I didn't notice anybody on any of the other boats. Either everyone was still asleep (an impossible assumption) or they were all still partying in Annapolis. A quick look behind our boat showed that the waves were smashing over the rocky bulkhead no more than 30 feet away.

Being the captain I attempted to install confidence by my usual calm demeanor. Thus, I screamed at the top of my lungs at my son, who had just finished fending off the sailboat, to start pulling up the anchor. At the same time I respectfully commanded my wife to attempt to fend off the two power boats (hell, if she could lift those doors by herself, she could push around 20,000 pound power boats).

Kay remained with the children, keeping them calm (or were the children were keeping her calm?).

Todd attempted to haul in the anchor but was making very little progress. It appeared that our anchor was still "set" and yet we were coming closer to the rocks behind us. To assist Todd I put the boat in motion towards the anchor line, therefore relieving the stress.

Todd hauled the excess anchor line in. We continued to do this with this large power boat at the front of our boat. Finally, we had the anchor line directly underneath us. At that moment the small power boat on our starboard side passed behind us and I threw the boat into reverse which pulled the anchor free.

Todd hauled the anchor up as I attempted to see where there might be a path through this chaotic mess of free floating boats in order to get out of the anchorage.

As Todd hauled in the anchor, Carole fended off both power boats (she did one hell of a job). She then immediately went to get some warm clothing (it was really cool for August, and all of us in pajamas).

Thankfully, I was now sitting in the helm seat, thus I no longer had to hold up my pajamas, allowing the use of both hands to steer the boat.

Todd spotted an opening between the boats. We carefully reversed our boat until we got close to the breakwater (the winds were really whipping up at this point) and gently steered our way through the maze of other boats.

The time was now approximately 1:00 a.m.

A Clear but Moonless Night

The night was beautifully clear. A major high pressure system was over the Chesapeake Bay. It was the time of a New Moon, and thus there was no moonlight.

Under such conditions the stars are remarkably clear. The sky was certainly dazzling although the darkness made the navigation difficult.

All of us on the boat were "high" from the excitement. We had survived!

Not only had we survived, but we had handled this emergency situation, in almost every respect, properly. (OK, so I yelled at my wife. Maybe as a captain I shouldn't have done that. But any married man can tell you that yelling at one's wife is a perfectly reasonable, rational occurrence.)

We headed down the Severn River towards the Chesapeake Bay. Because there was no moonlight, it was difficult to clearly see the obstacles, markers, and floating corks from the crab pots. Even so, our navigation proved faultless and we arrived back at our dock in approximately one hour and fifteen minutes.

At the Dock

We managed to get the boat into the boat slip without destroying either the dock or the boat. After tying the mooring lines we all realized that we were so wide awake from the experience it would be impossible to go to sleep so we did the next logical thing.

We opened up several bottles of wine, brought out the pretzel jar and sat up for over an hour feeling quite smug by having survived the ordeal.

*   *   *

EPILOG

And for those that are interested in the final details; no damage occurred to either my ying yang or my boat. But I did wonder, at my age, if my wife had a choice of where to have damage occur, would she have chosen my ying yang, or would she have chosen our new boat???

P.S.:   The next day Carole left the boat to go shopping for new pajamas with strong elastic. And I, on the sound advice from my ying yang, am sanding all the teak railings to ensure that there are no splinters.

CHAPTER 16

Wonderful Passaic

Amerca is often considered as a country of refugees. Oppressed poor people from all over the world continue to arrive in America to pursue "The American Dream."

In this quest for a better life, there are only a few cities such as Passaic, a city where immigrants or first generation Americans with limited education can find employment, a city that constantly strives to have an outstanding educational system so that children of these immigrants or first generation Americans can assimilate into the American dream. The school system provides the foundation for breaking down the barriers between cultures creating a common language and a common set of goals and friendships. The school system allows the new generation of America to pursue further studies and blossom and mature.

Historically, Passaic has done this difficult job in an admirable way. For example:

When I graduated from Passaic High in 1950, 378 out of 387 graduates were white.

One Hundred percent of the school board was white.

Eleven out of twelve school board members were males.

Approximately twenty-five percent of the high school class sent to college.

In the following half century the residents of Passaic profoundly changed. In many ways this was matched by the school board and the school system in the year 2000. For example: The year 2000:

The school board now has three Afro-American, five Latinos and only one person of European ancestry.

The public school population is now over ninety percent Latino and the city itself is estimated to have more than seventy-five percent of the population Latino.

The percent of graduates going to college is up to about forty-five percent.

What happened between 1950 and the year 2000? Very simple. Passaic did its job. It provided education, and thus, provided the American opportunity for its graduates. The graduates blossomed and achieved a more affluent way of life and moved out to the surrounding "bedroom communities." For example, of all the 1950 PHS graduates that responded to a questionnaire in the year 2000, 79% lived within fifty miles of the city of Passaic including 7% of them that still live in Passaic. This migration into the bedroom communities opened up the city to allow a large wave of new immigrants, those from Central and Latin America. The city adjusted, the school systems adjusted, and those immigrants will grow and prosper just like the previous generations grew and prospered. And they'll move out of the city and be followed again by poor immigrants from other parts of the world. That is the continuing role for Passaic.

I strongly objected when the New York Times recently described Passaic as a "grimy mill town." The Times has it totally wrong. Passaic is a heroic town performing an important fundamental part of the American Dream. It is providing the stepping stones for its youth to grow and blossom.

Certainly, this role for Passaic is not easy. It is not easy to have a significant portion of your population poor and working at near minimum wage jobs. It is also not easy to have the majority of city residents where

English is not the primary language. Moreover, it is not easy to have your industries grow obsolete and close.

However, the spark of Passaic has made each of these obstacles an opportunity, and Passaic has in the past and will in the future rise above these problems. That is the role of my Wonderful Passaic.

About the Author

Bob Rosenthal, besides being a prize-winning humor writer, is an eminent research engineer. He was a pioneer in the USA Apollo Space Program, a versatile inventor (holds over 40 US patents), a successful entrepreneur, and a university lecturer in over twenty countries. But he still leaves time to "smell the flowers."

Want more? www.wonderful-passaic.com

Mr. Cruise (as principal) - p.7
   Bill?
Teeterboro Airfield - p.14
Dr. Boone (Sup. of Sch.) - pp.35-36
Tulip St. Hebrew School - pp.36-
   Mr. Witte - p.36-38.39
      his love - 37-38.39
War effort
   Everyone involved - pp.41-42
      mother rolling bandages - p.42
      war bonds - war stamps p.42
      collecting newspapers pp.42-43
Paulison Ave. was on southern side, p.50
   of the part
Not Main Street, but Main Avenue - p.56 - corrected on p.58 > but refs.
                                                               back &
Erie R.R. came from Hoboken not Jersey City - pp.56-57   forth
Erie Station was not directly across
   from "skyscraper, but two blocks   } pp.56-57
   down... the address was 666 main or 333
Main Ave. did not run to Newark } p.58
   It stopped in Nutley
Coal cinders from trains - p.60
High school lunch wagons - p.69
Passaic High School - pp 69-
   Mrs. Card
   Auditorium - p.70
   Annex
   High standards p.71
   The "Y" - p.72
      Mr. "A" - pp.72-
      Mrs. Caskey
      Boverini
      Dr. Deaks - p.111
#74 & 112 busses - p 85
Ruth's Hut   pp 85-87 Ritz Ballroom - pp 87-88, 107
McKay's Orchids p.97
Shul on Hope Ave. - p.100
Ben Krone's (sp.?) - p.101
Ritz Restaurant } 103
Montauk Theater } 103
Pictures on inside of dixie-cup lids - 105
Julius Cinnamon (sp) Legue - 112
Morris Pashmein - 112

NYU in Bronx? - p. 115 - Engineering!
Phil Epstein pp. 119, 124
Curtis Wright - p. ~~125~~ 123
The Echo - p. 135
Most talkative - 137
grizzicle? - p. 141

9 780595 130474